Financial Freedom for Millennials & Gen Z

Building Wealth in a Post-Traditional Job Market

ETHAN WEALTHMORE

Table of Contents

Chapter 1: Redefining Financial Independence Today

For decades, the idea of financial independence has been closely linked to finding a stable, long-term job that offers a reliable paycheck. This belief has been deeply rooted in the minds of many, shaped by the economic conditions and societal norms of the 20th century. During this time, the industrial economy saw significant growth, marked by a variety of manufacturing and corporate roles that provided job security and a clear path toward retirement. The expectation of working for a single employer for most of one's career was not only common but actively encouraged. This era also featured widespread pensions and employer-sponsored retirement plans, creating a financial safety net that allowed individuals to plan confidently for a secure retirement.

Stable employment was a primary focus, and traditional financial wisdom recommended saving a specific percentage of income in conventional savings accounts. The common guideline suggested saving between **10%** and **20%** of one's income, a strategy that made sense when interest rates on savings accounts were much higher than they are today. People believed that consistent saving, combined with the power of *compound interest*, would lead to a comfortable retirement. This approach reflected a time when inflation rates were relatively low and the cost of living was more predictable.

Today, these traditional beliefs about financial independence are being reexamined as the job market and economy evolve. The rise of the **digital economy**, with its flexible work arrangements, gig opportunities, and non-traditional career paths, has fundamentally transformed the employment landscape. A 2020 report from the U.S. Bureau of Labor Statistics indicates a steady increase in the number of independent contractors and freelancers, highlighting a growing preference for flexibility and autonomy over the perceived security of a conventional 9-to-5 job.

The limitations of relying solely on stable employment for financial independence have become increasingly clear. The volatility of the global economy, underscored by events like the 2008 financial crisis and the disruptions caused by the COVID-19 pandemic, has revealed the fragility of traditional employment. Job security can no longer be taken for granted, and the idea of a "job for life" is quickly becoming a thing of the past. Adapting and diversifying income streams has become essential for achieving financial independence.

People are also reevaluating the traditional approach to saving, given today's economic realities. Interest rates on savings accounts have dropped to historic lows, making it less effective to save a fixed percentage of income in these accounts. Data from the Federal Reserve shows that the average interest rate on savings accounts in the United States has remained below **1%** for several years, making it challenging for savers to keep pace with inflation. As a result, many are exploring alternative investment opportunities that offer higher returns, such as:

- equities
- real estate
- digital assets like cryptocurrencies

Traditional beliefs about financial independence, rooted in past economic conditions and societal norms, now face significant challenges from the realities of today's digital, flexible economy. The notion that a stable, long-term job with a steady paycheck and saving a fixed percentage of income in traditional savings accounts are the best paths to financial security may no longer resonate with the current generation. Recognizing the limitations of these traditional paths and embracing new strategies that align with the opportunities and challenges of the modern economy has become essential.

The digital and flexible economy has emerged as a transformative force, reshaping how we perceive work and financial independence. At the heart of this shift is technology, which democratizes access to information and creates platforms that connect individuals with a diverse array of opportunities across the globe. The internet has become a powerful ally, enabling people to earn and invest in ways that were once beyond imagination, such as through online marketplaces and investment apps.

A significant development in this new economy is the rise of the gig sector. This model empowers individuals to take on short-term, flexible jobs, often facilitated by digital platforms that streamline the hiring process. Companies like **Uber**, **Lyft**, and **DoorDash** have become household names, providing the chance to earn income on one's own terms. Workers can select their hours and locations, making it easier to juggle other commitments like education or family responsibilities while still earning a living.

Remote work has gained substantial traction, particularly after the COVID-19 pandemic prompted many organizations to implement work-from-home policies. This experience demonstrated that productivity can thrive outside a traditional office, leading many companies to maintain remote options even after public health restrictions were lifted. For employees, this flexibility means they can perform their jobs from virtually anywhere, reducing commuting time and costs while fostering a healthier work-life balance. It also opens up job opportunities with companies in different cities or countries, expanding the range of available positions.

Freelancing has become an increasingly popular avenue, with platforms like **Upwork** and **Fiverr** connecting skilled professionals to clients seeking specific services. Freelancers can offer a wide array of services, including:

- Graphic design
- Writing
- Programming
- Marketing

This model allows individuals to leverage their skills to build a client base and generate income without being tied to a single employer. They can also juggle multiple projects simultaneously, which helps diversify their income streams.

These new work models provide both flexibility and autonomy, paving the way for multiple income sources. By combining different streams of income, individuals can mitigate financial risk and enhance their earning potential. For instance, someone might drive for a ride-sharing service on weekends, freelance as a graphic designer during the week, and invest in digital assets like cryptocurrencies. This approach fosters a more resilient financial plan that doesn't rely solely on one source of income.

Many have seized these opportunities to achieve financial freedom. Alex Fasulo, for example, built a six-figure income as a freelance writer by utilizing platforms like **Fiverr** to offer her services online, reaching clients worldwide and expanding her business beyond the confines of a traditional job. Entrepreneurs like Tim Ferriss advocate for a lifestyle centered on efficiency and flexibility, as illustrated in his *"4-Hour Workweek"* concept, which encourages a balance between financial success and personal fulfillment.

The digital and flexible economy encompasses both earning and strategic investing. Technology has simplified access to a wide range of investment options, from traditional stocks and bonds to innovative choices like peer-to-peer lending and real estate crowdfunding. Online platforms equip individuals with the tools and resources necessary to make informed investment decisions, granting them greater control over their financial futures.

Adaptability is essential for achieving financial independence in today's world. The ability to adjust and respond to changing circumstances is vital in an era defined by rapid technological advancements and fluctuating market conditions. This quality goes beyond merely switching jobs or acquiring new skills; it involves cultivating a mindset that views change as an opportunity for growth. For Millennials and Gen Z, who have navigated a fast-paced digital landscape, this perspective is a key component of their financial strategy.

A dedication to continuous learning is also a cornerstone of modern financial independence. The digital economy increasingly rewards those who actively seek education and skill enhancement. Online courses, webinars, and digital certifications have made it easier and more affordable to acquire new skills or deepen existing knowledge. Platforms like **Coursera**, **Udemy**, and **LinkedIn Learning** offer a diverse array of subjects, including:

- Programming
- Digital marketing
- Financial analysis
- Entrepreneurship

Embracing lifelong learning helps individuals remain competitive in the job market and adapt to industry changes.

Digital tools and platforms are now indispensable for wealth-building in the current economy. The internet has broadened access to financial markets and investment opportunities, enabling people to manage their finances more effectively than ever. Budgeting apps like **Mint** and **YNAB** (You Need A Budget) assist users in tracking their spending and savings goals. Investment platforms such as **Robinhood** and **Acorns** allow individuals to start investing with minimal amounts of money. These resources empower individuals to take charge of their finances and make informed decisions based on real-time data.

Creating a diverse portfolio of income sources is a savvy strategy for pursuing financial independence. Relying solely on one income stream can be precarious, especially in an unpredictable job market. Diversifying income through side hustles, online businesses, and innovative investment strategies helps establish a more robust financial foundation. Options include:

- Freelance work
- E-commerce
- Running an online business (e.g., selling on Etsy or Amazon or offering digital services)

These avenues can significantly enhance earning potential beyond traditional employment.

Emerging investment options, such as cryptocurrencies and peer-to-peer lending, present alternative avenues for wealth growth. Cryptocurrencies like **Bitcoin** and **Ethereum** have gained traction as digital assets with the potential for high returns, but they also carry considerable volatility and risk, making it essential to fully understand them before investing. Peer-to-peer lending platforms, including **LendingClub** and **Prosper**, enable individuals to lend money directly to borrowers, often yielding higher returns than conventional savings accounts or bonds. These strategies require thoughtful consideration and a willingness to explore new financial models.

Financial literacy and education are vital for navigating this evolving landscape. Grasping the fundamentals of personal finance, investing, and risk management is crucial for making informed decisions. Programs and resources from organizations like the **National Endowment for Financial Education** (NEFE) and the **Financial Industry Regulatory Authority** (FINRA) offer valuable insights and guidance. Enhancing financial literacy empowers individuals to better evaluate opportunities, manage risks, and make choices that align with their long-term objectives.

Creating a personalized financial strategy is crucial for successfully navigating the complexities of today's economy. Start by setting clear, achievable goals that align with your aspirations and current situation, using the **SMART** criteria: *specific, measurable, attainable, relevant,* and *time-bound.* For instance, instead of simply saying "save more money," specify your goal as "save $5,000 for an emergency fund within the next 12 months." This method provides clear direction and motivation, making it easier to track your progress and adjust as necessary.

Life changes and shifts in the economy can significantly impact your financial situation, so it's vital to revisit your goals regularly. Events like a job change, welcoming a new family member, or market fluctuations may necessitate updates to your strategy. Set aside time every few months, such as quarterly or twice a year, to review your progress and make any necessary adjustments. This practice keeps your plan aligned with your evolving needs and the broader economic landscape.

Exploring different income-generating activities and investments can help you find what works best for your lifestyle and risk tolerance. The modern economy offers a variety of opportunities, including:

- Side gigs
- Innovative investment options
- Freelance work

Dedicate a specific amount of time or resources to explore these possibilities—perhaps three to five hours a week for freelance work or a small investment like $500 in a new asset class. Keep an eye on the results and use your insights to refine your approach, aiming to enhance both returns and personal satisfaction.

Many individuals in the gig economy face the challenge of variable income, but strategic planning can help manage it effectively. Establish a baseline budget that covers essential expenses—such as housing, utilities, and groceries—based on your lowest expected monthly income. This ensures you can meet your obligations even during slower periods. Any earnings above this baseline can be directed toward savings, investments, or discretionary spending.

Sticking to a budget requires discipline, and digital tools can make the process easier. Apps like **Mint** and **YNAB** (*You Need A Budget*) assist in tracking income and expenses, categorizing spending, and identifying areas for improvement. With real-time insights into your finances, you can make informed decisions and stay focused on your objectives.

Digital tools are also invaluable for planning and tracking your progress toward financial independence. Investment platforms like **Robinhood** and **Acorns** provide easy access to a variety of assets, simplifying the process of building a diversified portfolio. These platforms often include educational resources and analytical tools to help you make informed investment choices. You might also consider using a financial dashboard or spreadsheet to consolidate all your data, giving you a clear overview of your assets, liabilities, and net worth.

Key Takeaway

Achieving financial independence today means moving beyond the old model of relying on a single, stable job and traditional savings. Millennials and Gen Z can thrive by diversifying income streams, embracing flexible work, and leveraging digital tools for earning and investing. Adaptability, continuous learning, and a personalized financial strategy are essential for building wealth in the modern, ever-changing economy.

Chapter 2: The Rise of Non-Traditional Careers

T he job market has undergone significant changes over the past few decades, shifting from traditional, stable employment to more dynamic and unconventional roles. This transformation largely results from the decline of manufacturing and industrial jobs, which once formed the backbone of the American economy. In the mid-20th century, these positions were abundant, providing steady work and decent pay for millions, with average hourly earnings around $25. However, as globalization intensified and technological advancements accelerated, the landscape began to evolve.

Globalization has been a major force in reshaping job markets. Companies have sought to reduce operational costs and enhance efficiency, leading to the outsourcing of many manufacturing roles to countries with much lower labor costs, such as **China** and **Mexico**. This shift resulted in a loss of about 5 million manufacturing jobs in the United States between 2000 and 2010 and also changed the nature of work itself. The focus transitioned from producing goods to delivering services, resulting in a significant increase in service-oriented positions. Today, the service sector dominates the U.S. economy, accounting for over 80% of GDP and encompassing a wide range of industries, including:

- healthcare
- education
- finance
- hospitality

Technological advancements have further accelerated this transition. The rise of the internet and digital technologies has created new opportunities and challenges in the job market. Automation and **artificial intelligence (AI)** now play a crucial role in many industries, streamlining operations and enhancing productivity. At the same time, these technologies have replaced certain roles, particularly those involving routine and repetitive tasks. Estimates indicate that up to 20 million manufacturing jobs could be automated by 2030. As machines and algorithms take over these tasks, the demand for human labor in these areas has decreased.

Automation and AI have not only impacted job availability but have also transformed the skills required in the workforce. There is now a heightened demand for expertise in:

- data analysis
- digital marketing
- software development
- other tech-focused fields

Businesses are collecting and analyzing vast amounts of data, projected to reach 175 zettabytes by 2025. The ability to interpret and leverage this information has become increasingly valuable. Data analysts and scientists are in high demand, tasked with extracting insights that inform decision-making and strategic planning.

Digital marketing has emerged as a crucial component of modern business. With the rapid growth of online platforms and social media, companies are investing more in engaging with customers in the digital realm. This trend has led to a strong demand for professionals skilled in strategies such as **search engine optimization (SEO)**, **content marketing**, and **social media management**. The digital marketing industry is expected to expand to $640 billion by 2027.

Software development is also experiencing remarkable growth. As technology continues to evolve, the need for skilled developers remains high, with job openings projected to increase by 22% from 2020 to 2030. These professionals design and maintain the software that powers everything from smartphones to enterprise systems. Coding and development skills are in high demand, creating a wide array of career opportunities.

Tech-based roles are expanding beyond data analysis, digital marketing, and software development. Fields like **cybersecurity**, **cloud computing**, and **AI research** are also growing rapidly. As reliance on digital technologies increases, businesses and individuals require cybersecurity experts to safeguard sensitive data and systems. Job openings in this field are expected to grow by 31% by 2029. Additionally, cloud computing specialists are in high demand as organizations transition their operations to cloud-based platforms to enhance flexibility and scalability.

Technology has been a game changer in the shift toward non-traditional jobs, transforming not only how work is accomplished but also how it's perceived. The internet, mobile devices, and cloud computing have broken down geographical barriers, enabling people to work remotely or embrace the lifestyle of digital nomads. With a dependable internet connection, individuals can work from virtually anywhere. High-speed internet—often exceeding **100 Mbps** in many urban areas—and affordable mobile technology facilitate collaboration with teams around the globe, participation in virtual meetings, and access to cloud-based resources without the need for a physical office. This level of flexibility is particularly appealing to Millennials and Gen Z, who often seek to harmonize work with personal interests and responsibilities, valuing remote options that support a more integrated lifestyle.

Cloud computing has revolutionized business operations by offering scalable and cost-effective solutions for data storage and processing. Companies can launch applications and services without hefty investments in physical infrastructure, fostering the growth of startups and small businesses. Technology has become increasingly accessible, lowering the barriers for entrepreneurs to compete with larger, established firms. For individuals, cloud-based tools like *Asana, Slack*, and *Google Workspace* streamline project management, communication, and collaboration, making it easier to juggle multiple gigs or freelance projects at once.

Cultural shifts have also played a significant role in the transition to non-traditional careers. Younger generations are increasingly prioritizing work-life balance, flexibility, and jobs that resonate with their values. Unlike previous generations, Millennials and Gen Z often place greater importance on experiences and personal fulfillment rather than just job titles or salaries. Many are drawn to careers that align with their beliefs and lifestyle preferences, opting for roles that provide meaningful engagement rather than solely financial rewards. The gig economy, which emphasizes flexibility and autonomy, is particularly attractive to those who want to tailor their work schedules around their personal lives.

A growing number of young professionals are inspired by the opportunity to make a positive impact on society or the environment, leading to an increase in social entrepreneurship and businesses focused on sustainability and social responsibility. Choosing projects and clients that reflect personal values serves as a strong motivator for those pursuing freelance or contract work, allowing them to support causes they care about while achieving financial stability.

Economic pressures, such as rising living costs and student debt, have also nudged more individuals toward non-traditional jobs. In many cities, the cost of living has skyrocketed—rent for a one-bedroom apartment in places like San Francisco or New York often exceeds **$3,000** a month—making it challenging for young professionals to cover basic expenses on a single income. Many are turning to side hustles and gig work to supplement their earnings, and these flexible roles enable individuals to work around their primary job or school commitments, providing extra financial security when needed.

Student debt is another pressing issue. With average student loan debt in the United States now surpassing **$30,000**, many Millennials and Gen Z are seeking alternative ways to earn money and manage their financial responsibilities. Freelancing or starting a small business can offer higher earning potential and greater financial independence, along with opportunities to develop new skills and expand professional networks, which can lead to better prospects down the line.

The landscape of non-traditional jobs is continually evolving, with several new categories gaining traction and offering Millennials and Gen Z a wide array of opportunities for financial independence. The **gig economy** stands out as a significant development, fundamentally transforming how people approach work. Roles in ride-sharing and delivery services have surged in popularity due to their flexibility and easy access. Platforms like **Uber**, **Lyft**, and **DoorDash** empower individuals to earn income on their own terms, providing a level of autonomy that traditional employment often lacks. These positions involve short-term engagements, allowing workers to choose their hours and workload, which makes it easier to balance other responsibilities or pursue additional income.

Freelance platforms now play a crucial role in this economy by connecting skilled professionals with clients seeking specific services. Sites such as **Upwork** and **Fiverr** have broadened the scope of freelance work, enabling individuals to offer services like:

- graphic design
- writing
- programming
- marketing

Freelancers can cultivate a diverse client base and manage multiple projects simultaneously, helping them create various income streams. By setting their own rates and selecting projects that align with their skills and interests, freelancing becomes an appealing and sustainable career path.

Online content creation has rapidly emerged as another major sector in the new economy. The growth of digital platforms has allowed individuals to transform their creativity and expertise into income. Blogging, podcasting, and video streaming are now viable careers, with platforms like **YouTube**, **Twitch**, and **Patreon** providing creators the tools to connect with audiences worldwide. Content creators earn money through advertising, sponsorships, and direct support from fans. Building a loyal audience and consistently producing engaging content are essential for success in this field.

E-commerce and digital entrepreneurship have opened even more doors in the new economy. The internet has eliminated many traditional barriers to starting a business, enabling individuals to create and sell products online without the need for a physical store. Platforms such as **Etsy**, **Amazon**, and **Shopify** simplify the process of launching an online shop, giving entrepreneurs the infrastructure to reach customers globally. This shift has empowered many to turn their passions into profitable ventures, whether selling handmade goods, digital products, or specialized services.

Digital entrepreneurship encompasses a wide range of innovative business models, such as:

- subscription services
- dropshipping

Subscription services provide a steady income, as customers pay regularly for access to products or services. **Dropshipping** allows individuals to sell products without maintaining inventory, as suppliers handle order fulfillment. This approach minimizes upfront costs and risks, making it a popular choice for those looking to enter e-commerce.

The landscape of non-traditional jobs is evolving quickly, and Millennials and Gen Z are uncovering a treasure trove of opportunities that come with significant perks. One of the most attractive features is the increased **autonomy** these roles offer. Unlike traditional employment, which often enforces rigid schedules and hierarchical structures, alternative positions empower individuals to set their own hours and choose their work environments. This flexibility allows for the pursuit of passion projects alongside primary responsibilities, fostering greater fulfillment and personal growth. For example, a freelance graphic designer can develop a personal art portfolio while managing client projects, seamlessly blending professional duties with personal aspirations.

Another key advantage is the ability to create multiple **income streams**. By engaging in various gigs or freelance assignments, individuals can strengthen their financial foundation. This strategy minimizes reliance on a single paycheck, which is particularly beneficial in an unpredictable job market. For instance, someone might earn income from:

- freelance writing

- operating an online store
- investing in digital assets

This effectively spreads financial risk and enhances overall earning potential.

However, these benefits come with their own set of challenges. Income instability is a significant concern. While traditional jobs typically provide steady pay, non-traditional roles can lead to fluctuating earnings, complicating financial planning and budgeting for monthly expenses. Establishing a financial safety net is essential. Setting aside a portion of income during high-earning months can help cover costs during slower periods. A practical strategy involves calculating average monthly income over a year and saving enough to cover three to six months of expenses in an emergency fund.

Another challenge is the absence of employer-sponsored benefits like health insurance, retirement plans, and paid leave. Those in non-traditional roles must take the initiative to secure these benefits independently. This may involve purchasing private health insurance or setting up a retirement account such as an *IRA* or *solo 401(k)*. It's important to factor these expenses into the overall financial plan to ensure long-term security.

Achieving success in non-traditional careers also hinges on strong **self-discipline** and effective time management. Without the structure of a conventional workplace, distractions and overwhelm can easily creep in. Establishing a routine with defined work hours, regular breaks, and time for personal development is crucial for maintaining productivity. Digital tools like project management apps and time-tracking software can be invaluable in organizing tasks and meeting deadlines.

Personal development is a powerful strategy for overcoming the challenges of non-traditional work. Continuing education and skill-building enhance marketability and open new doors. Online courses, workshops, and networking events enable individuals to stay current with industry trends and connect with potential clients or collaborators. Platforms like *LinkedIn* provide valuable opportunities to expand a professional network and showcase skills and achievements.

Tip

If you're considering a non-traditional career path, start by building a financial safety net. Set aside savings to cover at least three to six months of living expenses. This cushion will help you manage income fluctuations and reduce stress as you explore flexible work, side hustles, or entrepreneurship in the digital economy.

Flexible Work, Gig Roles, and Remote Job Opportunities

In today's fast-paced job market, flexible work arrangements, gig roles, and remote jobs have become vital components of the modern economy, offering a wealth of opportunities tailored for Millennials and Gen Z. These models shine for their adaptability, empowering individuals to customize their schedules and work environments to suit their personal needs and preferences. This flexibility is particularly appealing to younger generations who prioritize **work-life balance** and seek to harmonize their professional and personal lives.

Such arrangements cater to the diverse lifestyles of today's workforce. Unlike the traditional 9-to-5 setup, they enable individuals to select their working hours and locations. This autonomy allows for better management of personal commitments alongside professional responsibilities, often leading to increased satisfaction and productivity. Employees can create schedules that align with their peak performance times and obligations. For example, a parent might choose to work early mornings or late nights to accommodate childcare, while someone who thrives in the evening could start their day later.

The **gig economy** plays a significant role in this landscape by providing short-term, task-based jobs that allow workers to juggle multiple projects or roles at once. This model offers a variety of experiences and income streams. Those who crave variety and independence can thrive here, selecting projects that align with their skills and interests, and building a portfolio that showcases their strengths. Well-known platforms like *Uber*, *Lyft*, and *DoorDash* exemplify this concept, enabling individuals to earn money on their own terms by deciding when and how much they work.

Remote jobs have gained tremendous traction, especially after the COVID-19 pandemic highlighted the feasibility of working from home for many roles. Employees can now perform their duties from virtually anywhere, eliminating the daily commute and opening doors to global job markets. This shift allows individuals to work for companies around the world, broaden their career options, and reside in areas with lower living costs while still earning competitive salaries. For instance, a software developer in a rural area can work for a Silicon Valley tech company without needing to relocate.

The technology that supports these roles is crucial in making flexible work, gig roles, and remote jobs a reality. Collaboration tools like *Slack* and *Microsoft Teams* keep team members connected, no matter where they are. Project management platforms such as *Asana* and *Trello* help organize tasks and monitor progress, ensuring projects stay on track. Secure communication tools like *Zoom* and *Google Meet* provide reliable video conferencing for virtual meetings and presentations.

These technologies not only facilitate remote work but also enhance productivity and teamwork in traditional office settings.

Staying informed about industry trends and market demands is essential for identifying sectors where flexible work is on the rise. The tech industry, for instance, is rapidly expanding due to advancements in **artificial intelligence**, **cybersecurity**, and **software development**. The following fields are also experiencing robust growth:

- Digital marketing, as businesses increasingly rely on online platforms to connect with their audiences.
- Creative sectors like graphic design, content creation, and video production, which present numerous flexible opportunities due to their project-based tasks and remote collaboration.

A focused strategy is essential for identifying and assessing opportunities in flexible work, gig roles, and remote jobs. Begin your search on online platforms and job boards that specialize in non-traditional employment, such as **Upwork**, **Fiverr**, and **Remote.co**. These sites provide valuable resources for discovering freelance and remote openings. You can filter listings based on your skills, interests, and availability, making it easier to find roles that align with your career aspirations.

Professional networking sites like **LinkedIn** are crucial for building connections with industry professionals and uncovering job openings. Keep your profile updated to accurately reflect your current skills and experiences. Engage with content relevant to your field, join groups, and participate in discussions to expand your network and enhance your visibility to potential employers or clients. Networking goes beyond just finding job leads; it's about cultivating relationships that may lead to future collaborations or referrals.

Thoroughly researching potential employers or clients is vital. Investigate the company's mission, values, and culture to ensure they align with your own principles and career objectives. Websites like **Glassdoor** and **Indeed** offer employee reviews that provide insight into the work environment and management style. This information is invaluable in determining if a prospective employer aligns with your professional goals.

Establish clear criteria when evaluating job opportunities to ensure they meet your needs and expectations. Consider the following factors:
- Income potential and alignment with your financial goals
- Skill requirements to determine if you're qualified or if additional training is necessary
- Opportunities for advancement or skill development
- Work-life balance the position provides

Flexible work should support a healthy equilibrium between your professional and personal life.

Keeping your skills current is crucial for remaining competitive in the flexible job market. The digital economy evolves rapidly, so it's essential to maintain up-to-date skills for employability. Utilize online courses, webinars, and workshops to learn new skills or enhance existing ones.

Platforms like **Coursera**, **Udemy**, and **LinkedIn Learning** offer a wide range of courses, allowing you to tailor your learning to your career objectives.

A strong online presence and portfolio are key to attracting potential employers and clients. Your portfolio should clearly and appealingly showcase your skills, experiences, and achievements. Include concrete examples of your work, such as completed projects, published articles, or design samples, to demonstrate your capabilities. A well-organized portfolio highlights your expertise and helps you stand out from other candidates.

Maintain a professional online presence on social media by sharing industry-related content, engaging with thought leaders, and participating in relevant discussions. This approach boosts your visibility and establishes you as a knowledgeable and active professional in your field.

Succeeding in Flexible and Nontraditional Work Paths

How-To

Ready to launch your flexible career? Start by listing your top skills and passions, then match them to in-demand roles like freelancing or digital marketing. Set clear, SMART goals—such as landing your first client in three months. Build a standout online presence with a personal website and active social profiles. Keep learning through online courses, and use productivity tools to stay organized. Finally, create a budget that accounts for variable income and prioritize building an emergency fund.

Flexible work arrangements require a strategic and personalized action plan. Begin with a thorough self-assessment to identify your unique strengths, interests, and skills—this step is crucial for aligning your abilities with non-traditional job opportunities. Make a list of your core competencies and passions, and reflect on the tasks you excel at and the activities that bring you the most joy. This approach will help you pinpoint where you can add value in areas like the gig economy, freelancing, consulting, or entrepreneurship.

Once you've clarified your strengths and interests, dive into exploring various fields and industries that offer flexibility. The digital economy presents exciting opportunities in:

- Content creation
- Digital marketing
- Software development
- Online education

Freelancing platforms like Upwork and Fiverr can connect you with clients looking for your specific skills, while consulting roles allow you to leverage your expertise in a particular sector.

Entrepreneurship offers a chance to innovate and carve out your own niche, whether that means launching a startup or developing a side project.

With potential career paths in mind, craft a detailed plan that outlines your short-term and long-term goals. Define what success looks like in flexible work, and establish specific, measurable, achievable, relevant, and time-bound (**SMART**) objectives to keep you focused. For example, you might aim to secure your first freelance client within three months and work toward generating a steady income from multiple projects within two years.

A strong online presence is vital for showcasing your expertise and attracting clients. Create a professional website or blog to highlight your skills, experience, and portfolio—this acts as your digital business card and provides potential clients with a clear understanding of your services. Utilize relevant social media platforms for networking and marketing; **LinkedIn** is excellent for professional connections, while **Instagram** or **Twitter** may be more suited for creative fields.

Continuous skill development is essential for staying competitive and adaptable in a rapidly changing job market. Take advantage of online courses, workshops, and certifications to broaden your expertise and unlock new opportunities. Platforms like *Coursera, Udemy*, and *LinkedIn Learning* offer a diverse range of courses tailored to various industries. Regularly updating your skills ensures you stay ahead of industry trends and can meet the evolving needs of clients.

Establishing a structured work environment is key to supporting productivity and maintaining work-life balance. Whether you're working from home or in a co-working space, create a dedicated area that minimizes distractions and fosters focus. Adhere to a disciplined schedule for effective time management. When juggling multiple projects or clients, set clear boundaries and prioritize your tasks. Tools like *Trello* or *Asana* can help you organize your workload and meet deadlines.

Effective financial management is crucial for navigating variable income. Develop a budget that accommodates fluctuating earnings, and concentrate on saving and investing in resources that support your work. Budgeting apps like *Mint* or *YNAB* can assist in tracking expenses and maintaining financial stability. Building an emergency fund provides a safety net during slower periods, and smart investments can help your finances grow.

Chapter 3: Building a Solid Financial Foundation

Tip

Automate your savings to make building an emergency fund and reaching financial goals effortless. Setting up automatic transfers—whether from your paycheck or checking account—removes the temptation to spend and ensures you consistently invest in your future, even on a variable income. This simple habit is especially powerful for Millennials and Gen Z navigating gig work or side hustles, helping you stay on track without constant effort. Start small if needed, and increase contributions as your income grows.

Achieving financial independence begins with a strong foundation, and an emergency fund is essential for that stability. This fund serves as a safety net, protecting you from unexpected expenses like medical bills, car repairs, or sudden job loss. For Millennials and Gen Z, who often navigate the uncertainties of gig work and non-traditional career paths, having this protection is particularly crucial.

Start by establishing a clear savings goal for your emergency fund. Most financial experts recommend setting aside enough to cover three to six months of essential living costs. This amount provides a buffer for emergencies while allowing you to allocate funds toward other financial goals. To determine your target, take a close look at your monthly spending, including fixed expenses like:

- rent or mortgage
- utilities
- groceries
- transportation
- insurance

For instance, if your basic monthly costs total $2,000, aim for a fund between $6,000 and $12,000.

Once you have your target in mind, open a separate savings account specifically for this purpose. Keeping the money separate helps you resist the temptation to use it for non-emergencies. Look for a **high-yield savings account** with a competitive interest rate, so your savings can grow while remaining accessible when you need them.

Consider your contributions to your emergency fund as a fixed monthly expense, just like rent or utilities. Setting up automatic transfers from your paycheck ensures you consistently add to your savings, eliminating the risk of forgetting or deprioritizing this vital step.

While regular contributions are important, you can also enhance your fund by depositing any unexpected income, such as tax refunds or bonuses, directly into the account. Allocating a portion of side hustle earnings can further boost your savings. For example, if you earn an extra $500 from freelance work, consider putting part of that into your emergency fund. This strategy not only accelerates its growth but also fosters a habit of prioritizing savings.

Regularly review your target to ensure it aligns with your current financial situation. Increases in living expenses, such as higher rent or new insurance costs, should prompt you to adjust your goal. Changes in your personal life, like starting a new job or welcoming a growing family, may also necessitate updates to your emergency fund. Periodically checking in on your savings helps you determine if you need to save more or modify your target.

Setting clear financial goals is essential for building a solid financial foundation. Begin by categorizing your objectives into **short-term**, **medium-term**, and **long-term** goals.

- Short-term aims, like paying off high-interest debt or saving for a vacation, are typically achievable within a year.
- Medium-term objectives may involve accumulating funds for a down payment on a home or purchasing a car, usually taking one to five years.
- Long-term aspirations, such as investing for retirement or funding a child's education, extend beyond five years.

To turn these goals into actionable steps, apply the **SMART** criteria: **Specific**, **Measurable**, **Achievable**, **Relevant**, and **Time-bound**. Instead of a vague goal like "save money," aim for something more concrete, such as "save $10,000 for a down payment on a house within three years." This method clarifies the amount, allows you to track your progress, ensures the goal aligns with your financial situation, supports your desire to own a home, and sets a clear deadline.

Once you've defined your objectives, create a detailed financial plan that outlines how you'll achieve each one. Include timelines, required monthly savings, and investment strategies. For instance, to save for a down payment, calculate the monthly amount needed to reach your target within your chosen timeframe using this formula:

$$\text{Monthly Savings} = \frac{\text{Total Savings Goal}}{\text{Number of Months}}$$

If your goal is to save $10,000 in three years, you'll need to set aside about $278 each month:

$$\text{Monthly Savings} = \frac{10,000}{36} \approx 278$$

Support your objectives with effective money management systems. Start with a realistic budget that accounts for both **fixed expenses** (like rent and utilities) and **variable expenses** (such as dining out and entertainment). Track your spending for a month to gain insight into your habits, then use that information to create a budget that reflects your actual expenses while still allowing for savings.

Budgeting tools or apps like *Mint* or *YNAB* can help you monitor your spending and stay on track. These tools categorize expenses, highlight spending patterns, and send alerts when you're approaching budget limits. They also enable you to set savings goals and track your progress, making it easier to remain focused.

Set up automatic transfers to direct money toward each goal, ensuring steady progress. Automating your savings reduces the temptation to spend money intended for your objectives. For example, if your monthly savings target is $278, arrange for an automatic transfer from your checking account to a dedicated savings account each month. This approach simplifies the process and helps you consistently prioritize your financial goals.

Regularly review and update your financial plan to accommodate changes in income, expenses, or priorities. Life circumstances can shift, so your plan should remain adaptable. A salary increase might allow you to save more each month and reach your goals faster, while unexpected costs could necessitate a temporary adjustment to your savings rate.

Keep your financial objectives aligned with your broader aspirations by reassessing them periodically. When you achieve a short-term goal, consider redirecting those funds toward medium- or long-term objectives. This ongoing cycle of setting goals, planning, and reviewing keeps you focused and motivated as you work toward building wealth.

Building Sustainable Money Habits

To develop sustainable money habits, start by cultivating a mindset that prioritizes long-term financial health and independence. This journey begins with education. A solid understanding of personal finance principles is essential, starting with the basics like living below your means and grasping how **compound interest** works. Spending less than you earn creates a surplus for savings and investments, providing a financial cushion while fostering discipline and thoughtful planning.

Compound interest is a powerful tool for growing wealth, allowing your money to increase at an accelerating rate as you earn interest on both your original investment and the interest it generates. For instance, if you invest $1,000 at a 5% annual interest rate, compounded yearly, it will grow to about $1,628 after ten years. The longer you keep your money invested, the faster it grows, making it crucial to start early and contribute regularly.

Continue expanding your personal finance knowledge by seeking out resources that align with your goals. Consider the following options:

- Books, such as "The Millionaire Next Door"
- Financial podcasts, like "The Dave Ramsey Show"
- Online courses from platforms like Coursera and Khan Academy

These resources can enhance your understanding and provide practical advice for managing finances.

Regularly review your financial statements and track your net worth to stay informed about your situation and identify areas for improvement. Tools such as spreadsheets or financial management apps can assist you in monitoring your assets, debts, and overall net worth. This routine check-in equips you with the information needed to make informed choices and adjust your approach when necessary.

Adopt a disciplined approach to spending by clearly distinguishing between needs and wants. Ensure your discretionary spending aligns with your values and long-term goals. Essentials like housing, food, and healthcare should take precedence, while non-essentials such as dining out or luxury items should be evaluated carefully. By focusing on your needs and aligning spending with your goals, you can maintain control of your budget.

Before making purchases, take a moment to consider how they fit into your budget and whether they support your financial objectives. Reflect on whether the purchase aligns with your values and if it will provide lasting satisfaction. This practice helps curb impulse buys and encourages more intentional spending.

Make savings and investments a priority to build financial stability. Set aside a specific portion of your income for savings before addressing other expenses. Automate this process by directing money into high-yield savings accounts or investment options like index funds or retirement accounts to ensure consistent saving.

Patience and perseverance are vital for financial growth. Building wealth takes time and steady effort. Setbacks may occur, but maintaining a long-term perspective helps you stay focused on your objectives.

Accountability can enhance your commitment to financial independence. Share your goals with a trusted friend or join a supportive group that encourages each other's progress. This network provides motivation, advice, and encouragement to help you stay on track.

Chapter 4: Budgeting for Variable Income Streams

A budget that adapts to fluctuating income streams is crucial for anyone navigating the gig economy, freelancing, or juggling side hustles. Begin by calculating your average monthly earnings based on historical data. Review past income statements to identify patterns, such as peak months or seasonal dips, which will help you establish a reliable baseline for expected revenue. Recognizing these trends enables more accurate forecasting of periods with higher or lower income, simplifying your financial planning.

Once you've identified income patterns, categorize your expenses into **fixed** and **variable** types. **Fixed expenses**—like rent, utilities, and loan payments—remain constant each month and should be prioritized, as they represent mandatory outflows that must be covered regardless of income fluctuations. **Variable expenses**, which can change from month to month, include discretionary items such as dining out, entertainment, and travel. By distinguishing between these categories, you can focus on essential expenditures and pinpoint areas where spending can be trimmed if necessary.

Implementing a tiered budgeting system can enhance your financial flexibility. This approach organizes expenses into three groups:

- Essential: Basic living needs, such as housing, food, and transportation.
- Important: Expenses that support your overall well-being but aren't critical, like gym memberships or streaming subscriptions.
- Discretionary: Non-essential costs that can be adjusted based on your monthly income.

Understanding these categories helps align your spending with actual earnings, ensuring that essential needs are met first while managing discretionary spending wisely.

An **emergency fund** is a vital component of an adaptive budget, serving as a financial cushion during months with reduced earnings. Aim to save enough to cover three to six months of essential expenses. This safety net allows you to concentrate on long-term financial goals without the constant worry of unexpected costs derailing your plans.

Digital budgeting tools or applications can be invaluable for managing fluctuating income streams. These tools track income and expenses in real time, provide insights into spending habits, and promote financial discipline. Apps like *Mint* or *YNAB* offer features for setting budgets, tracking expenditures, and sending alerts when you approach spending limits. Utilizing these technologies gives you a clearer view of your finances and supports informed decisions about spending and saving.

Set aside a specific percentage of each paycheck for savings and investments to build wealth, even when your income varies. Consistently allocating part of your earnings to savings keeps you on track toward your financial goals. This habit is essential for long-term stability, and adhering to a set savings percentage helps create a solid financial foundation, even amid income fluctuations.

Regularly reviewing your budget is key to evaluating your financial health and making necessary adjustments. Schedule these reviews to assess income and expenses, identify areas for improvement, and implement changes that align with your current situation. Staying proactive keeps you informed about your finances and supports smart decisions regarding spending and saving.

Consider opening multiple bank accounts to manage your finances more efficiently. Having separate accounts for taxes, savings, and everyday expenses simplifies tracking and allocation, making it easier to oversee your financial activities. This method also ensures that funds are set aside for specific purposes, reducing the risk of overspending and enhancing organization.

When your earnings increase in certain months, prioritize paying down **high-interest debt**. This strategy alleviates financial pressure during leaner periods and bolsters your overall financial health. Reducing debt frees up more income for savings and investments, helping you achieve financial stability more quickly.

Creating Flexible Budgets for Variable Income

A personalized, flexible budget is crucial for navigating the unpredictable earnings that come with freelancing, gig jobs, or side hustles. Begin by identifying and categorizing your income sources in detail. Create a thorough list of all potential revenue streams, including:

- specific freelance projects
- various gig economy jobs
- any side hustles you take on

By analyzing the variability in your cash flow, you can better anticipate fluctuations and develop a more accurate financial plan.

Once you've clarified your income sources, establish a dynamic tracking system and update it at least weekly to reflect any changes in earnings. This practice allows you to make timely adjustments to your budget. Utilizing digital tools or financial management apps can help you automatically monitor your income and expenses, providing real-time insights into your financial status. These resources not only save time but also deliver accurate, actionable data for your financial decisions.

Incorporating **buffer zones** into your budget is another essential strategy for financial resilience. These financial cushions enable you to manage unexpected expenses or sudden income changes without compromising your stability. For example, setting aside *10%* of your monthly income as a buffer can create a safety net during leaner periods and enhance your overall security.

Expanding your income portfolio is vital for minimizing risk and boosting financial stability. Actively pursuing new streams reduces reliance on any single source and mitigates the impact of fluctuations in one area. This could involve:

- taking on additional freelance projects
- exploring new gig opportunities
- investing in passive income sources like dividend-paying stocks or rental properties

Scenario planning techniques can help you adapt to financial uncertainties by forecasting different income levels and preparing corresponding budget adjustments. Developing multiple budget scenarios based on projected income ranges allows for quick transitions as your financial situation evolves.

Automation tools can improve the consistency of your financial commitments. Automating bill payments and savings transfers ensures these essential tasks are completed on time, even when income varies. This strategy helps you avoid late fees and penalties while keeping you focused on your savings goals.

Remaining open to continuous learning and adaptation is crucial in today's rapidly changing economic landscape. Staying informed about market trends and emerging opportunities can help you optimize your income sources and make well-informed financial decisions. You might achieve this by:

- reading industry publications
- attending relevant webinars
- enrolling in online courses to enhance your skills and knowledge

Regular self-assessment is also key to managing variable income. Routinely reviewing your financial progress allows you to identify areas for improvement and refine your budgeting strategies to align with changing income patterns and personal goals. This could involve a thorough review of your budget every month or quarter, analyzing income and expenses, and making necessary adjustments to stay on track.

Digital Tools for Tracking Irregular Income

Tip

Before committing to a budgeting app, take advantage of free trials or demo versions. Test how well the tool integrates with your income sources, tracks expenses, and fits your workflow. This hands-on approach helps you find the best match for your unique financial needs.

In today's ever-evolving job market, where freelancing, gig work, and side hustles are on the rise, effectively managing irregular income streams is essential for achieving financial stability. A range of digital tools and applications are now available to help individuals track and organize earnings from various sources. These resources cater specifically to the needs of freelancers, gig workers, and side hustlers, offering features designed to simplify the complexities of handling variable income.

One key feature to prioritize in these digital tools is **real-time income tracking**. This capability allows users to view their earnings as they come in, providing an immediate snapshot of their financial situation. Real-time tracking empowers better decision-making regarding spending, saving, and investing. Apps like QuickBooks Self-Employed and Wave provide this functionality, enabling users to visualize their cash flow instantly. These applications connect directly to bank accounts and payment platforms, ensuring all income is recorded accurately and promptly.

Customizable income categories are also vital, allowing users to organize earnings by project, client, or type of work. This flexibility makes it easier to pinpoint the most profitable income streams and focus efforts where they can yield the best financial results. For example, FreshBooks allows users to create their own income categories, streamlining financial tracking according to individual preferences. This feature is particularly beneficial for those managing multiple projects, as it highlights which ones contribute most significantly to overall earnings.

Seamless integration with various income sources is another crucial aspect. Many freelancers and gig workers receive payments through platforms like PayPal, Stripe, and direct bank transfers. Tools that connect effortlessly with these platforms can consolidate all income data in one place, offering a comprehensive view of cash flow. Xero and Zoho Books excel in this area, providing connections to a wide array of payment platforms and financial institutions. This integration saves time and minimizes errors that can arise from manual data entry.

The design and usability of these tools are important as well. An intuitive, user-friendly interface enables individuals to get started without requiring extensive technical knowledge, which is especially beneficial for those without a finance or accounting background. Mint and Personal Capital are recognized for their easy-to-navigate interfaces, making them accessible to a broad audience. Their clear navigation and visual representations of financial data help users quickly grasp their financial position.

Having both mobile and desktop versions of these applications is also essential to accommodate different user needs and work environments. Many freelancers and gig workers are frequently on the move, so access to financial data on a mobile device is crucial. Meanwhile, desktop versions can offer more detailed views and additional features for thorough financial analysis. YNAB (You Need A Budget) and PocketGuard both provide mobile and desktop options, allowing users to manage their finances anytime and anywhere.

Selecting the right digital tool involves considering specific financial needs. For instance, those working with international clients will benefit from an app that supports multiple currencies and offers currency conversion. If your tax situation is complex, a tool with tax tracking and reporting features can save considerable time and effort during tax season.

Free trials and demonstrations are an excellent way to explore these tools and see how they fit into your financial management routine. Many applications allow you to test their features before committing to a subscription. This hands-on approach helps you discover the tool that best aligns with your needs and preferences.

Evaluating digital tools for managing irregular income requires careful consideration of their ability to automate data entry from various platforms. This feature is essential for freelancers and gig workers who frequently receive payments from multiple sources, such as **PayPal**, **Stripe**, and direct bank transfers. **QuickBooks Self-Employed** shines in this area, connecting with over 20 payment processors and bank accounts. It automatically captures and categorizes all income data in real time, significantly reducing the time and effort spent on manual entry while minimizing the risk of errors.

The ability to generate detailed income reports and insights is also crucial, especially for users who need to analyze trends and make informed budgeting decisions. **Wave**, for instance, offers robust reporting tools that enable users to:

- Track income over specific periods
- Identify peak earning months
- Examine cash flow fluctuations

These insights are invaluable for creating a flexible budget that can adapt to changing income levels and help allocate resources more effectively.

Expense tracking adds considerable value to these applications. **Mint**, for example, provides comprehensive tracking that allows users to categorize spending into areas like groceries, utilities, and entertainment, while also setting limits for each category. This approach helps maintain financial health by aligning expenditures with income and financial goals. **Mint** also features a goal-setting tool, empowering users to establish clear financial targets—such as saving *$2,000* for a vacation or paying off *$5,000* in debt—and track their progress over time.

Budget forecasting is another key function, and **YNAB** (*You Need A Budget*) excels in this area. It enables users to project future income and expenses based on historical data and trends. With this forecasting capability, individuals can prepare for financial challenges like seasonal income drops and adjust their budgets to stay aligned with their goals.

When comparing pricing models, it's important to consider both free and premium options. Many apps offer a basic version at no cost, which is ideal for those just starting with financial management. **Wave**, for instance, provides a free version with essential features like income tracking and basic reporting. Users who require advanced options, such as payroll management or detailed analytics, may need to upgrade to a paid plan, typically starting at *$20* per month.

QuickBooks Self-Employed, on the other hand, operates on a subscription model with a monthly fee. This grants access to a comprehensive set of features, including automatic mileage tracking and tax estimation tools. For those who need these additional features and seek a more complete financial management solution, this subscription can be a cost-effective choice.

Selecting the right digital tool hinges on individual needs and preferences. Users should reflect on which features are most important—automation, reporting, expense tracking—and weigh these against the tool's cost. A thoughtful evaluation will help identify the most cost-effective solution for financial management needs.

Choosing a digital tool to manage irregular income involves a careful look at features and integrations that boost usability. A vital element is the ability to sync with accounting software, which is especially helpful for freelancers and gig workers who need to keep their financial records accurate. Tools like **QuickBooks Self-Employed** and **Xero** connect effortlessly with popular platforms, enabling users to import and export financial data with ease. This setup not only streamlines bookkeeping but also ensures that financial information stays up-to-date and precise, helping to avoid errors when tax season rolls around.

Exporting data for tax purposes is another important function. Many digital tools allow users to generate tax reports or export data in formats that work seamlessly with tax software like **TurboTax**. This feature simplifies the filing process, saves valuable time, and reduces stress. For instance, **Wave** includes a tax report function that gathers all necessary financial data into one convenient document, making tax preparation a breeze.

Security is paramount when dealing with financial information. Users should ensure that their chosen app employs strong security measures to protect sensitive data. Look for tools that offer:

- Encryption
- Two-factor authentication
- Regular security updates

Mint and **Personal Capital**, for example, are well-regarded for their robust security protocols, giving users peace of mind that their financial information is safe from unauthorized access.

Good customer support and community resources significantly enhance the user experience with any digital tool. A responsive customer service team can help with technical issues or provide guidance on how to make the most of the app's features. Community resources such as tutorials, forums, and user groups also offer valuable tips and insights from fellow users. **YNAB**, for instance, has a vibrant online community and a wealth of educational resources, including webinars and workshops, to help users unlock the app's full potential.

Selecting the right tool hinges on your specific needs, the complexity of your income sources, and your financial goals. If your income is straightforward, a basic app with essential features may be all you need. However, for those with multiple income streams or more complex finances, it's wise to opt for a tool that offers advanced features like detailed reporting and integration options. Make sure the app can cater to your unique financial situation and support your long-term objectives.

Individuals looking for automation and simplicity might gravitate toward apps like **QuickBooks Self-Employed** and **Wave**, which provide user-friendly interfaces and automated features to streamline financial management. On the other hand, those who need detailed analysis and forecasting should consider tools like **YNAB**, which offer comprehensive budgeting and forecasting capabilities.

Chapter 5: Managing and Paying Off Debt

Tip

When listing your debts, don't just jot down the basics—add details like interest rates, due dates, and minimum payments. Use a spreadsheet or a free app to keep everything organized and updated. This clear overview not only helps you spot which debts are costing you the most, but also makes it easier to track your progress and stay motivated. A well-organized debt list is your first step toward financial freedom.

U nderstanding the specific terms and conditions associated with different types of debt is essential for maintaining your financial well-being, especially for Millennials and Gen Z who often face the challenges of student loans and credit cards. Each type of debt has its own set of rules, interest rates, and repayment terms, all of which can greatly influence your financial stability. For example, federal student loans typically have interest rates ranging from 3.73% to 6.28%, which are generally lower than the average credit card rates that can soar above 20%. While student loans can accumulate significant amounts over time, credit card debt can escalate quickly due to compounding interest. By grasping the details of each type of debt, you empower yourself to make informed borrowing and repayment decisions that will positively impact your credit score and future financial opportunities.

Start your journey to managing debt by creating a comprehensive list of all your outstanding obligations. Include the following details:

- Creditor's name
- Total amount owed
- Interest rates
- Minimum monthly payments
- Due dates

This list will give you a clear overview of your financial responsibilities and serve as the foundation for a focused repayment strategy. Consider using a spreadsheet or a financial management app to keep everything organized and easily accessible.

Once you have your debt inventory, determine which obligations to tackle first by employing strategies like the **avalanche** or **snowball** method. The avalanche method prioritizes debts with the highest interest rates, potentially saving you a significant amount on interest payments over time. This approach minimizes the total interest paid, as illustrated by the formula $I = P \times r \times t$, where I represents interest, P is principal, r is the interest rate, and t is time. By paying off high-interest debts first, you can reduce the overall interest owed.

Conversely, the snowball method focuses on eliminating the smallest debts first. Paying off these smaller amounts quickly can boost your motivation and help you stay committed to your repayment plan, which is particularly beneficial if you need that extra encouragement to keep going. Both methods have their advantages, and the best choice will depend on your unique financial situation and what inspires you to stay on track.

Consolidating debt can also be a smart move, especially if you're juggling multiple high-interest obligations. Merging these into a single loan with a lower interest rate can simplify your payments and may reduce the total interest you pay. Additionally, don't hesitate to negotiate with creditors about lowering interest rates or setting up better payment plans. Many creditors are open to negotiation if you show a genuine commitment to paying off your debts.

Maintaining a regular repayment schedule is crucial to avoid missed payments, which can negatively impact your credit score and increase future borrowing costs. Set up automatic payments or reminders to ensure you never miss a due date. A strong credit score plays a vital role in your ability to borrow, the interest rates you receive on future loans, and even your job prospects in certain fields.

To reduce future borrowing, start with a realistic budget that accounts for all your expenses and income. Building an emergency fund is also essential, allowing you to handle unexpected costs without relying on credit. Explore alternative financing options, such as *scholarships*, *grants*, or *interest-free installment plans*, to lessen your dependence on loans.

Student loans present their own set of challenges, but understanding your options can simplify the process. Choose a repayment plan that aligns with your financial situation, whether it's **standard**, **graduated**, or **income-driven**. Familiarize yourself with **deferment** and **forbearance**, which can provide temporary relief during difficult times, and check if you qualify for loan forgiveness programs, particularly if you work in public service or similar fields.

Chapter 6: Smart Saving Strategies for Young Adults

Tip

Automating your savings—even if you start small—can be a game changer for building wealth. Set up automatic transfers to a high-yield savings or investment account right after payday. This "pay yourself first" approach helps you stay consistent, even when life gets busy.

C lear, achievable financial goals are the backbone of effective saving strategies, especially for young adults navigating a shifting job market.

Establishing these objectives creates a structured approach that steers financial decisions and keeps you focused on your long-term plans. Start by identifying both short-term and long-term aims, such as:

- Building an emergency fund
- Saving for a significant purchase
- Investing for retirement

Short-term goals typically span a few months to a couple of years and may include saving for a vacation, purchasing a new gadget, or establishing an emergency fund. This fund is essential as it serves as a financial safety net for unexpected expenses like medical bills or car repairs. Many experts recommend saving enough to cover three to six months of living expenses, providing a buffer against sudden financial challenges.

Long-term goals extend over several years and often necessitate substantial financial planning, such as buying a home, funding higher education, or preparing for retirement. Starting to invest early allows you to harness the power of **compound interest**, which can significantly grow your retirement savings over time.

To make these objectives actionable and effective, apply the **SMART** criteria. Goals should be **Specific**, **Measurable**, **Achievable**, **Relevant**, and **Time-bound**. This method brings clarity and motivation, transforming vague intentions into concrete plans. For example, instead of simply aiming to *save more money*, a SMART goal would be *save $5,000 for an emergency fund within the next 12 months by setting aside $417 each month*.

A personalized financial roadmap outlines the steps needed to achieve your goals. Begin with a candid assessment of your current financial situation, including income, expenses, and existing savings. This evaluation serves as your starting point for planning. Next, prioritize your objectives based on urgency and importance. For instance, if you lack an emergency fund, building one should take precedence over saving for a vacation.

Once you've established your priorities, break each goal into smaller, manageable steps. For retirement savings, this might involve opening a retirement account like a *401(k)* or *IRA* and setting up automatic contributions. For short-term goals, consider opening a separate savings account to keep funds organized and minimize the temptation to spend.

Regularly reviewing and updating your objectives is crucial, as life changes—such as a new job, relocation, or family growth—can alter your financial priorities. Dedicate time every few months or at least once a year to assess your progress and make any necessary adjustments. This practice ensures your financial plan remains aligned with your current needs and future aspirations.

Digital tools and apps can be invaluable for tracking progress and maintaining accountability. Budgeting apps like *Mint* or *YNAB (You Need A Budget)* allow you to set financial goals, monitor spending, and receive alerts when you approach your budget limits. These features provide real-time insights into your finances and empower you to make informed decisions.

Financial dashboards consolidate information from all your accounts, offering a comprehensive view of your situation. This makes it easier to identify trends, spot potential issues, and celebrate achievements. Many apps also enable you to set specific goals and visually track your progress, which can enhance motivation.

Sharing your goals with a trusted friend or joining a financial community can boost accountability. Connecting with others who share similar objectives can provide support, encouragement, and valuable advice. Online forums, social media groups, or local meetups focused on personal finance are excellent venues to find like-minded individuals.

Automating savings is a smart strategy that can greatly enhance your financial discipline and ensure you consistently contribute toward your goals. By setting up automatic transfers from your checking account to specific savings or investment accounts, you reduce your dependence on willpower, which can waver when faced with daily spending temptations. This method streamlines the saving process and guarantees steady progress toward a secure financial future without the need for constant oversight.

To kick off your automatic transfers, start by reviewing your monthly budget to identify a realistic amount to save regularly. Consider this figure a non-negotiable expense, similar to paying a utility bill, and embrace the principle of **"paying yourself first."** By prioritizing savings in this manner, you ensure that your financial goals receive funding before you spend on non-essential items. Most banks and financial institutions provide recurring transfer options through their online banking systems, allowing you to select the frequency—**weekly**, **bi-weekly**, or **monthly**—that best aligns with your income schedule and targets.

When choosing savings vehicles, seek out options that maximize your growth potential. Consider the following:

- High-yield savings accounts for short-term goals or emergency funds, offering interest rates significantly higher than traditional accounts.
- Online banks often provide these accounts with better rates due to their lower operational costs.
- For long-term objectives, consider micro-investing platforms like Acorns or Stash, which enable you to invest small amounts in diversified portfolios, capitalizing on the stock market's growth over time.
- Many of these platforms feature convenient options like round-ups, where your purchases are rounded up to the nearest dollar, and the difference is invested, making it easy to start investing without needing a large initial sum.

Freelancers and gig workers often deal with fluctuating income, which can complicate the automation of savings. To navigate this, implement a **percentage-based transfer system** instead of a fixed amount. By saving a consistent percentage of your income, your contributions will automatically adjust with your earnings. For example, if you save **10%**, earning $3,000 one month would mean saving $300, while earning $4,000 the next would result in $400 saved. This approach keeps your savings proportional to your income and helps maintain financial stability during variable periods.

Regularly reviewing and updating your automatic savings plan is crucial to ensure it aligns with any changes in your financial situation or goals. Life events such as a salary increase, a new job, or shifts in expenses may necessitate a reassessment of your strategy. Periodic evaluations help ensure your efforts are in sync with your current needs and future aspirations.

To make the most of your limited resources, start with a strategic budgeting plan that prioritizes essential expenses and pinpoints specific areas for savings. Begin by categorizing your costs into two main groups: **needs** and **wants**.

Needs encompass crucial expenses like:
- housing (rent or mortgage)
- utilities (electricity, water, gas)
- groceries (basic food items)
- healthcare (insurance premiums and out-of-pocket medical costs)

Wants, on the other hand, include discretionary spending such as:
- dining out
- entertainment subscriptions
- luxury items

By clearly separating these categories, you can ensure that your essential needs are met before allocating any leftover funds to non-essentials.

Creative budgeting methods can help you stretch your finances even further. The **zero-based budget**, for instance, assigns every dollar of your income a specific purpose, ensuring that your income minus expenses equals zero. This approach encourages you to track every dollar, which helps minimize wasteful spending and enhances your savings. The **50/30/20 rule** is another effective guideline: allocate 50% of your income to needs, 30% to wants, and 20% to savings and debt repayment. This structure promotes balance and keeps saving a top priority.

Reducing living costs is essential for maximizing your resources. Consider negotiating recurring bills like cable, internet, and insurance—many providers are willing to offer discounts or better rates, especially if you mention competitive offers from other companies. Cashback apps such as *Rakuten* or *Ibotta* can also help you earn rebates on everyday purchases, effectively lowering your overall expenses.

Embracing a minimalist lifestyle can lead to significant savings as well. By focusing on quality over quantity and eliminating unnecessary items, you can reduce both clutter and costs. This approach fosters mindful spending, where each purchase is intentional and purposeful, paving the way for a more sustainable financial future.

Taking on side hustles or freelance work is another great way to boost your income, especially when earnings fluctuate. Websites like *Upwork*, *Fiverr*, and *TaskRabbit* connect you with clients looking for skills in areas like graphic design, writing, or handyman services. Set clear goals for your side work, such as dedicating a specific number of hours each week or targeting a certain income, to maximize these opportunities.

Building a strong professional network can also enhance your earning potential. Attend industry events, join online forums, and connect with others in your field to uncover new opportunities and potential collaborations. Expanding your network can lead to referrals, partnerships, and even job offers, all of which can positively impact your financial outlook.

Community resources can provide valuable support for your financial goals. Many local organizations offer free financial literacy workshops, counseling, and educational programs to help you develop better money skills. Libraries, community centers, and non-profits often host these events, providing practical advice on budgeting, saving, and investing. Online resources like webinars and podcasts can further broaden your knowledge and keep you informed about the latest financial strategies.

Chapter 7: Creating and Diversifying Income Streams

How-To

Ready to turn your skills into income? Start by listing your top 5 strengths and passions. Research online platforms like Upwork or Skillshare to see how others monetize similar talents. Reach out to a mentor or peer for honest feedback on your list. Next, choose one skill to focus on and outline a simple plan: define your target audience, set a small goal (like landing your first client), and schedule time each week to build your portfolio. Take action— progress beats perfection!

Reaching financial independence starts with a thoughtful self-assessment to pinpoint which skills, passions, and interests can be transformed into income. Taking the time to reflect on these elements is crucial for identifying opportunities that align with your values and lifestyle, ensuring you stay motivated and fulfilled over time. Begin by evaluating your current abilities and interests, concentrating on activities you enjoy and excel at, as these often hold the greatest potential for generating income.

To gain a clearer understanding of your strengths, consider utilizing online skill assessments. Platforms like **Skillshare** and **LinkedIn Learning** provide targeted courses and evaluations that can help uncover your natural talents or strong interests. These resources offer insights into your current skills and highlight areas for growth, which is particularly important in today's rapidly evolving digital landscape.

Feedback from peers or mentors can also be instrumental in identifying potential income streams. Those familiar with your abilities can provide valuable insights into your strengths and suggest areas for improvement. They may recognize talents you've overlooked or propose innovative ways to leverage your skills. Mentors, in particular, can share their experiences and offer guidance on transforming a passion into a sustainable business.

Exploring hobbies or activities that could evolve into business ideas can be highly effective. Many successful entrepreneurs have found financial success by identifying niche markets or unmet needs related to their interests. For example, if you have a knack for photography, you might consider offering event services or selling prints online. If writing is your forte, think about content creation or freelance writing. The key is to discover where your interests intersect with what people are willing to pay for.

Aligning income opportunities with your values and lifestyle is vital for sustaining motivation and satisfaction. If flexibility and independence are important to you, consider the following options:

- Freelancing
- Launching your own business
- Seeking roles in the green economy

If sustainability is your passion, seek roles with companies committed to environmental responsibility. Choosing income streams that resonate with your core values enhances your chances of remaining dedicated and enthusiastic about your work.

Certain skills are particularly valuable in the digital marketplace, unlocking profitable opportunities. For instance, **graphic design** is in high demand and can lead to freelance work on platforms like **Upwork** or **Fiverr**. **Content creation**—encompassing writing, video production, and social media management—is also highly sought after, as businesses strive to enhance their online presence. Skills like **coding** and **digital marketing** are essential as well, with numerous online platforms offering freelance gigs or side projects.

To maximize these skills, join online platforms that connect freelancers with clients. Websites like **Upwork**, **Fiverr**, and **Freelancer** enable you to offer services, build a portfolio, gain practical experience, and establish a reputation in your field. These platforms also grant you the freedom to select projects that align with your interests, providing greater autonomy and control over your career trajectory.

Remember that the digital economy evolves quickly, so staying informed about industry trends is crucial. Regularly updating your skills and knowledge will help you remain competitive and adapt to market changes. This might involve:

- Taking online courses
- Attending webinars
- Engaging in industry forums

These activities will help you keep abreast of new developments.

After identifying potential income streams, it's time to put them into action by crafting a detailed business plan. This plan should clearly outline your objectives, define your target market with demographic and psychographic insights, include a comprehensive competitive analysis, detail your marketing strategies, and provide financial projections with specific revenue targets and expense estimates. A well-structured business plan acts as your **strategic compass**, guiding your decisions and keeping you focused on your goals. It also provides a framework for tracking progress through measurable milestones and allows for adjustments based on performance metrics.

In today's digital economy, having a professional online presence is crucial. Start with a website that effectively presents your services, showcases your portfolio with high-quality images and detailed descriptions, and makes your contact information easy to find. Opt for a clean, modern design that reflects your brand's identity and values, and ensure your site is mobile-friendly, as over half of web traffic comes from these devices. Launching a blog or vlog to share industry insights and expertise can help position you as a thought leader and attract potential clients.

A strong portfolio is essential for demonstrating your skills and experience. Include:

- High-quality examples of your best work
- Client testimonials that highlight specific outcomes
- Relevant certifications or awards that bolster your expertise

Tailor your portfolio to showcase the skills and services most relevant to your audience. If you're just starting out and lack extensive professional experience, consider adding personal projects or volunteer work that effectively showcase your capabilities.

Building relationships and increasing visibility within your industry requires proactive networking. Engage with your community both online and offline. Attend industry conferences, workshops, and networking events to connect with potential clients and collaborators. Online, join professional groups on platforms like *LinkedIn*, participate in relevant forums, and interact with industry leaders on social media. A robust network can lead to referrals, partnerships, and valuable insights into emerging trends.

To attract clients, focus on marketing your skills and services effectively. Utilize social media platforms to expand your reach. Tailor your content for each platform; for instance, share visually engaging content on *Instagram* and post professional updates and in-depth articles on *LinkedIn*. Consistency is key, so develop a content calendar to plan and schedule your posts. Engage with your audience by responding to comments and messages promptly.

Online marketplaces such as *Upwork, Fiverr,* and *Etsy* provide additional avenues for reaching potential clients. Create comprehensive profiles that highlight your skills, experience, and unique selling points. Use high-resolution images and clear, compelling descriptions to differentiate your offerings. Encourage satisfied clients to leave positive reviews, as these can enhance your credibility and attract new business opportunities.

Personal branding is a vital component of your marketing strategy. Define your **unique value proposition** and communicate it clearly across your website, social media profiles, and marketing materials. A strong personal brand distinguishes you from competitors and builds trust with potential clients.

Setting realistic timelines and goals for your ventures helps you stay focused and track your progress. Apply the **SMART criteria**—Specific, Measurable, Achievable, Relevant, and Time-bound—to establish clear objectives. Break larger goals into smaller, actionable tasks, assign deadlines to each, and regularly review your progress against these benchmarks. Adjust your strategies as needed to remain aligned with your objectives.

Diversifying income streams is a smart strategy to minimize financial risk and enhance economic stability, particularly in today's unpredictable job market. By establishing multiple sources of revenue, individuals can build a solid financial foundation and respond more effectively to market changes. This approach not only provides a safety net during economic downturns but also opens doors for growth and innovation.

One effective way to diversify is by identifying complementary opportunities that leverage your existing skills and interests. For example, if you have expertise in a specific area, you might consider creating digital products like **e-books**, **online courses**, or **webinars**. These offerings can generate passive income while also establishing your authority in the field. Platforms such as *Teachable* and *Udemy* simplify the process of creating and selling courses, giving you access to a global audience and the potential to earn significant income from each course.

Teaching online courses is another excellent option, especially with the e-learning sector expanding rapidly and a growing demand for knowledgeable instructors across various subjects. Whether your expertise lies in **coding**, **graphic design**, or **personal finance**, sharing your knowledge can lead to both personal fulfillment and financial gain. Websites like *Skillshare* and *Coursera* provide robust platforms for course creation and marketing, enabling you to earn extra income on a flexible schedule.

A subscription-based service can also deliver consistent revenue while fostering customer loyalty. Consider what unique value you can offer on a recurring basis, such as:

- Exclusive content
- Personalized coaching
- Curated product selections

This model is effective across industries like fitness, wellness, technology, and entertainment, with potential monthly revenues ranging from hundreds to thousands of dollars.

Effective time management is crucial when juggling multiple projects. To prevent burnout, prioritize tasks based on urgency and importance. Project management tools like *Trello* or *Asana* can help you organize your workload and set achievable deadlines. Breaking larger projects into smaller, manageable tasks keeps your progress steady and helps you avoid feeling overwhelmed. Remember to schedule regular breaks and downtime to maintain your productivity.

Regularly assessing and adjusting your income sources is essential for maximizing profitability and ensuring they align with your personal and financial goals. Conduct periodic reviews to evaluate the performance of each stream. Focus on key metrics such as revenue, customer feedback, and market trends to pinpoint areas for improvement. This approach empowers you to make informed decisions about where to concentrate your efforts and resources.

Consider these steps for effective evaluation:

- Set clear benchmarks for success, such as specific revenue targets or customer acquisition goals.

- Gather comprehensive data on each stream, including sales figures, expenses, and customer feedback.
- Analyze the data to identify patterns, strengths, and weaknesses.
- Make adjustments based on your findings, such as reallocating resources or refining your marketing strategy.

Chapter 8: Roadmap to Launching and Scaling Side Hustles

Tip

Before diving into your side hustle, spend time in online communities like Reddit, LinkedIn, and Facebook groups related to your interests. These spaces offer real-world insights, highlight unmet needs, and connect you with potential collaborators or mentors—often before trends hit the mainstream.

Achieving financial independence starts with discovering a profitable side hustle, and this journey begins with thorough research, which is the cornerstone of any successful venture. Understanding market trends, consumer demands, and emerging industries is essential for aligning potential hustles with your unique skills and interests. This strategic match not only boosts your chances of success but also keeps the work engaging and personally rewarding.

Begin by diving into industry reports to gain crucial insights into current market dynamics and future forecasts. These documents often spotlight growth sectors and emerging trends, providing a clear framework for identifying new opportunities. For example, the surge in remote work has increased demand in areas like **digital marketing**, **e-commerce**, and **online education**. Spotting these trends early positions you to take full advantage of them.

Online forums and social media groups are treasure troves of information. Platforms like *Reddit*, *LinkedIn*, and *Facebook* host vibrant communities where professionals and enthusiasts discuss trends, share experiences, and offer advice. Engaging in these groups gives you real-time feedback and a deeper understanding of consumer needs and preferences. They can also uncover unmet market demands, giving you a chance to shine.

Conducting a competitive analysis is a vital step in the research process. By examining existing businesses in your chosen field, you can identify market gaps and areas for differentiation. Consider the following elements during your analysis:

- Product offerings
- Pricing strategies
- Customer reviews
- Marketing tactics

This analysis can reveal opportunities for you to provide something unique or enhance current solutions. For instance, if competitors receive negative feedback about customer service, prioritizing exceptional support could set you apart.

Once you have a potential side hustle in mind, validating the idea before committing significant resources is crucial. Surveys are an effective way to gauge interest and gather feedback from your target audience. Utilize tools like *SurveyMonkey* or *Google Forms* to create surveys that inquire about potential customers' needs, preferences, and willingness to pay for your product or service. The insights you gather will help you refine your offering and ensure it aligns with market demand.

Testing a **minimum viable product** (MVP) is another excellent method for validating your idea. An MVP is a streamlined version of your product or service that allows you to test core features with minimal investment. Launching one enables you to collect user feedback, pinpoint areas for improvement, and make necessary adjustments before scaling up. This approach mitigates risk and helps ensure your final product is well-received.

Small-scale pilot tests are also valuable for assessing demand and feasibility. These trials allow you to experiment with your side hustle in real-world conditions, offering insights into operational challenges and customer interactions. For instance, if you're considering a food delivery service, start by offering it to a small group of friends or family. This initial run helps you refine logistics, pricing, and customer service before expanding to a broader audience.

Staying updated on industry developments and committing to ongoing education are essential for enhancing and adapting your venture over time. The business landscape is ever-changing, and keeping ahead of trends gives you a competitive advantage. Subscribe to industry newsletters, attend webinars, and participate in workshops to keep your knowledge fresh. Continuous learning empowers you to adjust your approach as needed and seize new opportunities as they arise.

Once you validate your side hustle idea, the next step is to create a detailed and actionable plan for launching it. Set specific, measurable objectives to guide your efforts and keep you on track. Make sure these goals align with your long-term financial aspirations, ensuring they are both ambitious and achievable. For instance, if your goal is to earn an extra **$1,000** per month within six months, break this down into smaller, quantifiable milestones, such as:

- Acquiring five new clients each month
- Completing three projects weekly

A clear definition of your venture's scope helps maintain focus and ensures your efforts are strategically directed toward your objectives. Identify your target audience by analyzing their demographics, preferences, and pain points. This understanding allows you to tailor your offerings effectively. For example, if you provide graphic design services, determine whether your audience consists of small business owners, startups, or individuals with personal projects, and adjust your marketing strategies accordingly.

Your **value proposition** sets you apart from competitors and convinces potential clients to choose your services. Define what makes your side hustle unique—whether it's your specialized expertise, the quality of your work, or the personalized service you offer. Highlight these strengths in all marketing materials to attract and retain clients.

Selecting the right **business structure** is a key decision that impacts your legal obligations, tax responsibilities, and personal liability. Options include:

- Sole proprietorships
- Partnerships
- Limited liability companies (LLCs)
- Corporations

Each structure has its own pros and cons. Research these thoroughly and choose the one that best aligns with your business goals and risk tolerance. For example, an LLC offers personal liability protection and flexible tax options, which appeals to many entrepreneurs.

Legal compliance is crucial to avoid potential pitfalls. Depending on your venture, you may need specific permits or licenses. Check the regulatory requirements in your area and industry to ensure you operate within the law. Familiarize yourself with your tax obligations, such as self-employment taxes, and consider consulting a tax professional to help navigate these complexities.

A professional online presence builds credibility and attracts clients. Create a website that showcases your services, portfolio, and contact information. Ensure the design is clean, user-friendly, and mobile-optimized. Set up social media profiles on platforms like *LinkedIn*, *Instagram*, or *Facebook* to increase visibility and connect with potential clients. Consistent branding across all platforms reinforces your professional image and builds trust with your audience.

Branding plays a major role in distinguishing your venture from others. Develop a cohesive brand identity that reflects your values and resonates with your target audience. This process includes designing a logo, choosing a color scheme, and establishing a consistent tone of voice. Consistency in branding across your website and social media strengthens recognition and appeal.

Technology and digital tools help streamline operations and boost efficiency. Use project management tools like *Trello* or *Asana* to organize tasks and track progress. Accounting software such as *QuickBooks* or *FreshBooks* simplifies financial management. Analytics tools allow you to monitor performance metrics, such as website traffic or social media engagement, so you can identify effective strategies and areas for improvement.

Networking and building relationships within your industry should be a priority as you prepare to launch. Attend relevant events, participate in online forums, and connect with other professionals to expand your network and gain valuable insights. These connections can lead to collaborations, referrals, and new opportunities that support your growth.

To effectively scale a side hustle, it's crucial to establish systems and processes that can handle increased demand while upholding high-quality standards. **Automating** routine tasks is key in this regard. By leveraging technology, you can streamline operations and free up valuable time for growth initiatives. For instance, *customer relationship management (CRM)* software can manage follow-ups and simplify client interactions, while *accounting software* takes care of invoicing and financial tracking. Automation not only boosts operational efficiency but also minimizes the risk of human error, ensuring consistent service delivery across all customer touchpoints.

Outsourcing non-core activities is another vital strategy for scaling. By delegating tasks that don't directly contribute to your business's unique value, you can concentrate on strategic growth areas that drive revenue. For example, hiring a virtual assistant to handle administrative tasks or partnering with a marketing agency for promotional campaigns allows you to focus on product development and enhancing customer engagement. This approach optimizes resource allocation and brings in specialized expertise that can significantly elevate your performance.

Customer feedback and performance metrics are invaluable for pinpointing areas for improvement and potential expansion. Regularly gathering feedback through structured surveys or direct communication reveals insights into customer needs and preferences, helping you refine your offerings. Performance metrics, such as:

- Conversion rates
- Customer retention rates
- Sales growth percentages

provide quantitative insights into your overall health. Reviewing these metrics highlights successful strategies and areas needing attention, guiding your decisions on where to allocate time and resources most effectively.

Forming partnerships or collaborations can greatly enhance your market reach and service offerings. Aligning with complementary businesses or industry influencers opens doors to new audiences and allows you to leverage shared resources for mutual benefit. For example, a graphic designer might collaborate with a web developer to create comprehensive branding packages, or a fitness coach could team up with a nutritionist to deliver integrated wellness programs. These partnerships not only expand your market presence but also increase the value of your services, making them more appealing to prospective clients.

Reinvesting profits back into the business is essential for fostering development and innovation. Allocating funds to expand product lines or enhance marketing initiatives drives growth and increases market share. For instance, investing in targeted digital advertising can significantly boost your brand visibility, while developing new products or services can attract a broader customer base. Additionally, investing in skills development, such as attending industry-specific workshops or enrolling in relevant online courses, keeps you competitive and responsive to evolving industry trends.

Strategic planning and regular goal assessments ensure your side hustle remains aligned with changing market conditions and personal aspirations. Establishing clear, measurable objectives provides both direction and motivation, while periodic reviews allow you to evaluate progress and make necessary adjustments. This ongoing evaluation process helps maintain agility in response to market trends and shifts in consumer behavior, ensuring you stay relevant and competitive.

Chapter 9: Investing Basics and Low-Risk Strategies

Tip

Start investing with as little as $5 using modern apps that offer fractional shares. This lets you own pieces of high-value stocks like Amazon or Tesla without needing a big upfront investment. Automate your contributions to build wealth consistently and take advantage of dollar-cost averaging. Choose platforms with low fees, educational resources, and strong customer support to make your investment journey smoother. Remember, consistency and learning are key—don't wait for the "perfect" moment to begin. The sooner you start, the more time your money has to grow.

I nvesting is a powerful tool for building wealth and achieving financial independence, especially in today's rapidly evolving digital economy. To invest successfully, it's essential to have a solid understanding of the fundamental concepts that guide smart decisions. This involves familiarizing yourself with key terms and grasping the main types of investments that every beginner should know.

Stocks represent ownership in a company. When you purchase a stock, you own a piece of that business and have a claim on its profits and assets. While stocks can offer high returns, they also come with increased risk due to their value fluctuating significantly based on company performance, market trends, and the overall economy. This volatility means that while stocks can lead to substantial growth, they can also result in considerable losses.

Bonds operate differently. They are essentially loans made to corporations or governments, and in return, you receive regular interest payments and get your principal back when the bond matures. Generally viewed as safer than stocks, bonds provide steady income and are less affected by market fluctuations. However, this safety often translates to lower returns compared to equities.

Mutual funds gather money from multiple investors to create a diversified portfolio of stocks, bonds, or other securities. Professional fund managers oversee these investments, offering both diversification and expert guidance. This makes mutual funds appealing for beginners, although they do come with management fees and may not always outperform benchmark indices.

Exchange-Traded Funds (ETFs) also hold a mix of assets like mutual funds, but they can be bought and sold on stock exchanges just like individual stocks. Typically, they have lower fees and provide more flexibility, making them an excellent choice for those looking for diversification without the higher costs associated with mutual funds.

Diversification is crucial in investing. Spreading your money across different asset classes helps mitigate risk. Maintaining a mix of stocks, bonds, and other investments reduces the impact if one area underperforms. The saying "Don't put all your eggs in one basket" perfectly captures this principle. A diversified portfolio can help smooth out returns and shield you from significant losses.

A clear understanding of the **risk-reward relationship** is essential for effective investing. Investments that promise higher returns usually come with higher risk. For example, stocks have historically outperformed bonds but are more volatile, while bonds offer greater stability but lower returns. Finding the right balance between risk and reward depends on your personal financial goals and your comfort level with risk.

Setting realistic financial goals and timelines shapes your investment strategy. You might aim to save for a home, fund a child's education, or build a retirement nest egg. The timeline for each goal will influence your investment choices. Short-term objectives may require safer, more liquid options like bonds or money market funds, while long-term aspirations might make stocks more attractive due to their potential for greater growth over time.

Risk tolerance is a personal consideration. You need to assess how much risk you can handle and how you respond to market fluctuations. Factors such as age, income, financial responsibilities, and investment experience all play a role. A younger individual with a steady income and few obligations might be willing to take on more risk for higher returns, while someone nearing retirement may prioritize capital preservation and opt for safer investments.

Before diving into investing, it's important to conduct a thorough review of your financial situation. Take stock of your income, expenses, debts, and savings. A clear understanding of your finances will help you determine how much to invest and which strategies align with your needs. This self-assessment will guide you toward the best investment approach for your goals and circumstances. Patience, discipline, and a commitment to continuous learning are vital for success in investing.

To begin investing with small amounts of money, leverage modern platforms and apps that have revolutionized the investment landscape. These tools allow you to purchase **fractions of shares**, so you don't need to buy a whole share at once. This is especially advantageous for those with limited funds, as it opens the door to high-value stocks like *Amazon* or *Tesla* without requiring thousands of dollars upfront. Popular options for fractional investing include:

- Robinhood
- Stash
- Acorns

All of these feature user-friendly interfaces and low minimum investment requirements.

The first step in your investment journey is to open a **brokerage account**. This account gives you access to the stock market and enables you to buy and sell securities. To set it up, you'll need to provide personal information such as your Social Security number, employment details, and financial background. Most platforms offer a quick and straightforward online application that takes just a few minutes. Be sure to choose the type of account that aligns with your financial goals.

Taxable accounts provide the most flexibility, allowing you to withdraw funds at any time without penalties, although taxes will apply to dividends or capital gains. **Individual Retirement Accounts (IRAs)** offer tax advantages for retirement savings. Traditional IRAs allow for tax-deductible contributions, while Roth IRAs enable tax-free withdrawals in retirement. **Employer-sponsored 401(k) plans** are another excellent option, often featuring matching contributions that can boost your savings. Understanding the differences between these accounts and their tax implications is crucial for making informed investment decisions.

Account fees and charges can significantly affect your returns, so it's important to understand them before opening an account. Common fees include:

- Trading commissions
- Account maintenance fees
- Expense ratios for mutual funds and ETFs

Some platforms, like *Robinhood*, do not charge commissions, which is a great benefit for beginners with limited funds. However, always review the details, as some apps may have hidden fees or higher expense ratios.

Choosing a trustworthy brokerage or investment app involves considering several factors. An easy-to-use interface is essential, especially for newcomers. Access to educational resources can enhance your understanding of investing and improve your decision-making, so look for platforms that offer tutorials, webinars, and articles on various investment strategies. Reliable customer support is also key; ensure the platform provides assistance through phone, email, or live chat. Additionally, keep an eye on transaction costs, as high fees can eat into your returns if you trade frequently.

Setting up **automatic contributions** helps cultivate investment discipline and takes advantage of **dollar-cost averaging**. Automating your investments means you'll consistently add to your portfolio, regardless of market conditions. This strategy reduces the temptation to time the market, which can be risky and often leads to poor outcomes. Dollar-cost averaging involves investing a fixed amount at regular intervals, helping to smooth out the effects of market fluctuations. For example, investing $100 each month allows you to buy more shares when prices are low and fewer when prices are high, potentially lowering your average cost per share over time.

Minimizing risk is crucial when investing small amounts, as it safeguards your capital while fostering growth. **Asset allocation** is a smart strategy that involves spreading your investments across various asset classes—like equities, fixed income, and cash equivalents—to strike a balance between risk and return. This method helps mitigate the negative effects of any single underperforming asset on your overall portfolio. For those just starting out, low-cost index funds or exchange-traded funds (*ETFs*) provide a straightforward way to achieve diversification. These funds track specific indices, such as the S&P 500, offering broad market exposure that lessens the risks tied to selecting individual stocks.

Index funds and ETFs present several benefits for beginners compared to individual stocks. Their inherent diversification spans a wide array of securities, effectively distributing risk across multiple assets. Moreover, these funds typically have lower expense ratios than actively managed options, as they require less oversight. This cost efficiency can enhance your returns over time, particularly with smaller investments. Their ease of buying and selling also adds liquidity and flexibility to your portfolio management.

Regularly reviewing and rebalancing your portfolio is vital for maintaining your desired asset allocation. Over time, the values of different assets can shift, potentially causing your portfolio to deviate from its original mix. For instance, if stocks surge, they may represent a larger portion of your portfolio than intended, heightening your risk. Rebalancing involves:

- Selling some assets that have appreciated significantly
- Purchasing more of those that have underperformed
- Realigning your portfolio with your targets

This practice helps manage risk and keeps your investments in sync with your financial goals.

Staying informed about market trends and economic indicators is essential for making sound investment decisions. Economic factors like interest rates, inflation, and employment statistics can greatly influence market performance. For example, rising interest rates can lead to declining bond prices, while high inflation can diminish purchasing power. Keeping an eye on these indicators allows you to anticipate market shifts and adjust your investment strategy accordingly.

Successful investing relies on continuous learning and adaptation. Financial markets are always evolving, so staying updated on new developments can give you an advantage. Subscribing to reputable financial news sources, attending webinars, or engaging in investment forums can broaden your knowledge. Connecting with others who share your interests can also provide valuable insights and support as you navigate your investments.

Technology plays a significant role in enhancing your investment strategy. Many platforms now offer tools and features that help track market trends and analyze portfolio performance. These resources provide real-time data and alerts, making it easier to respond swiftly. Some platforms even include educational materials, such as articles and tutorials, to deepen your understanding of investing.

As you gain experience and confidence, you may choose to increase your investment amounts and explore more advanced strategies. Always keep your **risk tolerance** and **financial goals** in mind. Balancing the pursuit of higher returns with prudent risk management ensures that your investment approach remains aligned with your long-term objectives.

Investing presents both psychological and financial challenges, making it essential to maintain a long-term perspective. This mindset empowers individuals to navigate the inevitable market fluctuations without letting emotions steer their decisions. Emotional reactions can often lead to impulsive actions that jeopardize financial goals. For example, during market downturns, the temptation to sell off investments to avoid further losses can be intense, but giving in to this impulse typically results in locking in losses rather than allowing investments the opportunity to bounce back.

Behavioral biases frequently influence decisions in this field. The fear of missing out (**FOMO**) can drive investors toward the latest trends or popular stocks, often resulting in purchases at inflated prices. Sticking to a well-defined strategy and understanding that not every opportunity aligns with financial goals can help mitigate **FOMO**. Loss aversion, where the desire to avoid losses overshadows the pursuit of gains, may lead individuals to cling to losing investments longer than they should, hoping to break even. Acknowledging this tendency and establishing clear exit strategies can help lessen its impact. Overconfidence is another prevalent bias, causing individuals to overestimate their knowledge or ability to predict market movements, which can lead to taking on excessive risk. Regularly reviewing performance and seeking feedback from trusted advisors can foster a balanced and realistic approach.

A disciplined investment plan with clear objectives helps maintain focus, even amid market volatility. This plan should detail financial goals, risk tolerance, and investment timelines, providing a structured framework for decision-making. Sticking to the plan requires commitment and the ability to overlook short-term market fluctuations. Periodic reviews ensure that the plan remains aligned with evolving financial situations and objectives.

Investment tracking tools and performance metrics are invaluable for monitoring progress toward financial goals. These resources provide insights into portfolio performance, making it easier to identify trends and make informed adjustments. Metrics such as:

- Return on investment (ROI)
- Asset allocation
- Risk-adjusted returns

offer a comprehensive view of investment health. Celebrating small achievements along the way can enhance motivation and reinforce positive financial habits. Whether reaching a savings milestone or achieving a target return, recognizing these successes helps sustain momentum.

Guidance from financial advisors or mentors offers valuable perspective. These professionals can share insights on market trends, assist in refining investment strategies, and provide reassurance during uncertain times. Engaging with a community of investors who share similar interests also fosters support and accountability. Sharing experiences, challenges, and successes with others cultivates camaraderie and encourages disciplined investing.

Community support plays a crucial role in maintaining investment discipline. Joining investment clubs or online forums creates opportunities to exchange ideas and learn from others' experiences. These groups provide diverse perspectives and strategies, keeping individuals informed and motivated. Interacting with people who have similar financial goals offers encouragement and accountability, reinforcing commitment to the investment plan.

Chapter 10: Navigating Digital Assets and New Investments

Tip

Before diving into digital assets, set clear investment goals and assess your risk tolerance. Start small—allocate only what you can afford to lose, and diversify across different asset types. Always use secure digital wallets and enable two-factor authentication to protect your holdings. Staying updated on market trends and regulations will help you make smarter, safer decisions in this fast-evolving space.

Digital assets have emerged as a dynamic force in the financial landscape, creating a wealth of opportunities for investment and wealth building.

Unlike traditional investments such as stocks and bonds, these assets include a variety of innovative instruments, such as cryptocurrencies, NFTs (Non-Fungible Tokens), and tokenized securities. Each category possesses unique traits that set them apart from conventional financial products.

Cryptocurrencies like Bitcoin and Ethereum function as digital currencies on decentralized networks that leverage **blockchain technology**. This technology ensures transparency and security by recording transactions on a distributed ledger that is immutable and accessible to all network participants. While these currencies can yield impressive returns due to rapid price increases, they also carry significant risks, including extreme price volatility and shifting regulatory landscapes that may influence their legality and usage.

NFTs represent a unique category of digital assets. These tokens are singular and indivisible, often representing ownership of digital art, music, or other creative works. Unlike cryptocurrencies, which can be exchanged on a one-to-one basis, NFTs are distinct and cannot be traded equally. This uniqueness has driven their popularity in the art and entertainment sectors, offering fresh avenues for monetizing digital creations.

Tokenized securities introduce another innovative type of digital asset. These traditional financial instruments, such as stocks or bonds, have been digitized and issued on a blockchain platform. Tokenization enables fractional ownership, enhances liquidity, and may reduce transaction costs. However, the regulatory framework for these securities is still developing, which can pose challenges for investors who must navigate compliance and legal considerations.

Blockchain technology underpins digital assets, providing a secure and transparent method for recording transactions. It has the potential to transform established financial systems and unlock new investment opportunities. However, the nascent stage of this technology also brings risks, including security vulnerabilities and the possibility of regulatory actions that could affect market stability.

Investing in digital assets offers several advantages, such as the potential for high returns and increased portfolio diversification. These investments can grant access to emerging markets and technologies that may boost overall performance. Yet, these benefits come with notable risks. The volatility of these assets can result in significant price fluctuations, and the absence of clear regulatory guidelines can create uncertainty for investors. Security threats, including hacking and fraud, also present serious risks to asset safety.

Thorough research and evaluation are crucial for navigating these challenges. Developing a solid understanding of the underlying technology, keeping an eye on market trends, and verifying the credibility of projects are essential steps for making informed investment choices. **Digital wallets** are vital for safeguarding assets. These wallets can be hardware-based, offering offline storage, or software-based, providing convenience and easy access. Implementing security features like two-factor authentication and cold storage options can significantly enhance protection against theft and loss.

Embarking on an investment journey in digital assets requires thoughtful planning. Choosing a reliable exchange is essential to ensure a secure and trustworthy platform for buying and selling. It's also important to understand the fee structures associated with trading and transferring these assets, as these costs can directly impact overall investment returns. Adopting strong security practices, such as using complex passwords and enabling two-factor authentication, is critical for safeguarding investments.

Staying informed about regulatory changes and market developments is vital for making sound investment decisions. The digital asset sector evolves rapidly, and shifts in regulations or market conditions can significantly affect investors. Starting with a modest allocation to these assets, while considering personal risk tolerance and investment objectives, can help mitigate potential losses while still providing exposure to this fast-paced market.

Comparing Crypto, Crowdfunding, and Alternative Investments

Tip

Before diving into digital assets, set clear financial goals and risk limits. Start small, diversify your investments, and never invest money you can't afford to lose. Research each platform and asset thoroughly—especially in crypto and crowdfunding—since volatility and illiquidity are common. Staying informed and disciplined will help you navigate new opportunities while protecting your financial future.

In the fast-evolving world of digital assets and investment opportunities, Millennials and Gen Z aiming for financial independence must grasp the unique features of **cryptocurrency**, **crowdfunding**, and **alternative investments**. Each of these avenues offers distinct opportunities and challenges, necessitating a thoughtful approach to optimize potential returns while effectively managing risks.

Cryptocurrency is a digital or virtual currency secured by cryptographic techniques and operates on decentralized networks utilizing **blockchain technology**. This framework removes the need for a central authority, like a bank, to validate transactions. Investors in assets such as Bitcoin and Ethereum can experience significant returns, often fueled by rapid price increases. However, these profits come with considerable volatility, as prices can fluctuate dramatically in short timeframes due to market sentiment, regulatory shifts, and technological advancements. To mitigate these risks, consider the following strategies:

- Diversify holdings by spreading investments across various coins and tokens to distribute risk.
- Establish clear investment limits and adhere to them to prevent impulsive decisions during turbulent times.

Crowdfunding broadens investment opportunities for a larger audience, enabling individuals to support innovative projects and early-stage companies through platforms like Kickstarter and Indiegogo. This method allows investors to back projects they are passionate about, with the potential for substantial returns if the project thrives. However, the risk of project failure remains high, and liquidity is often limited, making it challenging for investors to sell their stakes. To navigate these challenges, it is crucial to assess:

- The credibility of the project.
- The experience of the founding team.

- The market potential.

Conducting thorough due diligence helps pinpoint projects with a higher likelihood of success. Look for well-defined business plans, realistic financial forecasts, and strong alignment with market demands. Engaging with the project team can also yield valuable insights into its viability.

Alternative investments cover a wide array of non-traditional assets, including real estate crowdfunding, peer-to-peer lending, and collectibles. These options provide avenues to generate income and diversify beyond conventional stocks and bonds. Consider the following alternative investment options:

- Real estate crowdfunding enables investors to pool resources for property investments, making markets accessible without hefty upfront costs.
- Peer-to-peer lending connects borrowers with individual lenders, creating opportunities for attractive returns through interest payments.
- Collectibles, such as artwork or rare coins, can appreciate over time, offering another path to wealth accumulation.

However, these investments carry their own risks, including market illiquidity, which can complicate the quick sale of assets, and valuation challenges that make determining an asset's true worth difficult. To evaluate these investments, research the platform's reputation, understand the underlying asset, and review historical performance data. Careful due diligence helps identify opportunities that align with your financial goals and risk tolerance.

Chapter 11: Building Your Personal Brand Online

In today's digital landscape, building a strong personal brand online is crucial for attracting the right opportunities, clients, and revenue streams. The first step in this journey is to create a strategy that clearly defines your **unique value proposition**. This involves a thoughtful analysis of your skills, passions, and experiences to pinpoint the qualities that set you apart in your field. Take some time to reflect on your areas of expertise, the topics that excite you, and how your past experiences have shaped your professional perspective. This self-assessment will empower you to develop a value proposition that is both authentic and compelling.

Once you have a solid grasp of your unique value, the next step is to precisely define your target audience by identifying the specific demographics, interests, and challenges of the individuals you want to reach. Tailoring your messaging to resonate with this group is essential, which means using language, tone, and content that directly address their aspirations and pain points. Aligning your brand message with the specific needs of your audience fosters a connection that is both meaningful and impactful.

A consistent online presence is key to reinforcing your identity. Establish a cohesive visual and verbal identity across all platforms, including social media, personal websites, and professional networks. Consistency in elements like:

- Color palette
- Logo
- Tagline

boosts recognition and contributes to a strong image. This approach ensures your online presence genuinely reflects your brand's personality and values, making it easy for your audience to identify and connect with you.

To amplify your brand, leverage social media effectively by choosing platforms that align with your audience's preferences and your professional goals. For instance, *LinkedIn* is great for professional networking, while *Instagram* excels in visual storytelling. Post content regularly, engage with your followers, and utilize analytics to refine your strategy. These insights will help you understand which types of content resonate most with your audience, allowing you to adjust your approach for greater impact.

Content creation and curation are vital components of personal branding. Producing original material that showcases your expertise—such as blog posts, videos, or podcasts—positions you as a thought leader in your industry. Sharing relevant industry content not only demonstrates your knowledge but also keeps your audience informed about current trends. A blend of original and curated content enhances your credibility and builds trust.

Networking and collaboration can significantly expand your reach and influence. Engage with influencers and peers in your field through thoughtful comments, shares, and collaborative projects. Participate in virtual events and webinars to connect with potential clients and partners. These interactions boost your visibility and open doors to new opportunities and collaborations.

Maintaining your brand requires regular updates to your online profiles and portfolios to highlight new skills and accomplishments. Keep an eye on your online reputation and respond constructively to feedback to maintain a positive image. Ongoing attention ensures your brand remains relevant and continues to resonate with your audience.

To monetize your brand, explore various income opportunities such as:

- Affiliate marketing
- Sponsored content
- Offering services and digital products

Your brand can attract freelance projects, consulting roles, or speaking engagements, creating multiple revenue streams. Leveraging your influence helps you build a sustainable income that aligns with your passions and expertise.

Trust and credibility are the cornerstones of a successful personal brand. Consistently provide value, stay transparent, and fulfill your commitments to cultivate a loyal audience and client base. Trust develops over time through actions and interactions that demonstrate your dedication to meeting your audience's needs and interests.

Chapter 12: Automating Savings, Investments, and Planning

STYLE

Setting, seamless ambiance with gentle sste, repeating pallect rhythm and ease.

Pursuing financial independence becomes much more achievable when Millennials and Gen Z automate their savings and investments. Technology makes it easy to set up systems that help reach financial goals with minimal manual effort, allowing more time and energy for other important aspects of life and career.

A simple way to automate savings is by establishing automatic transfers. Online banking platforms and financial apps enable users to schedule regular transfers from checking accounts to savings or investment accounts. Choose a percentage of income that can be comfortably saved each month—let's say **15%**—and set it up to move automatically to a high-yield savings or investment account. This method ensures consistent saving and fosters disciplined habits without the hassle of managing the process every month.

Robo-advisors also make investing automation a breeze. These platforms use advanced algorithms to manage portfolios based on individual risk tolerance and financial goals. After entering preferences like risk level and investment timeline, the robo-advisor creates a diversified portfolio tailored to your needs and automatically rebalances it to maintain the desired asset allocation and enhance tax efficiency. This way, users enjoy the benefits of professional investment management without the hefty fees that come with traditional financial advisors.

Numerous savings apps and tools can further boost saving effectiveness. Some apps round up purchases to the nearest dollar and deposit the difference into a savings or investment account. For instance, if a coffee costs $3.75, the app rounds up to $4.00 and puts $0.25 into savings. Over time, these small amounts can add up, helping to grow savings with minimal effort. Budgeting apps can also assist in tracking expenses and pinpointing areas for cutbacks, offering insights into spending habits and enabling smarter financial decisions.

Employer-sponsored retirement plans like **401(k)s** provide another excellent method for automating savings. By enrolling in these plans and setting up automatic contributions, individuals can take advantage of tax-deferred growth and, in many cases, employer matching contributions. Employer matching is essentially free money that can significantly enhance retirement savings. For example, if an employer matches **50%** of contributions up to **6%** of salary, contributing at least **6%** ensures you receive the full match, boosting your overall savings rate. Automatic contributions to a 401(k) facilitate consistent retirement saving and allow you to benefit from compound interest over time.

Financial planning software is essential for streamlining management tasks. These tools are crafted to improve budgeting, goal setting, and progress tracking, while also giving you a clear view of your financial landscape. By bringing all your accounts together on one platform, these applications provide real-time insights into your spending habits, making it simpler to spot areas where you can cut costs and redirect funds toward your goals. For example, programs like **Quicken** or **Personal Capital** categorize expenses into:

- housing
- transportation
- entertainment

This organization enables a thorough review of monthly spending, which is vital for making informed decisions and aligning your expenditures with long-term objectives.

Setting up notifications and alerts is another important element of effective management. Most banking apps and financial software offer customizable alerts for various account activities. You can create notifications for:

- upcoming bill payments

- low balances
- unusual transactions that might signal fraud

These alerts help ensure timely payments and prevent costly overdraft fees. Push notifications also keep you updated on your account status and significant milestones, serving as reminders of your progress and helping you stay motivated to stick to your financial plan.

Tax automation simplifies financial management for both individuals and businesses. Tax software like **TurboTax** or **H&R Block** connects with your accounts to handle calculations and submissions automatically. This integration allows the software to gather relevant data, ensuring your returns are accurate and up to date. It also helps track deductible expenses throughout the year, making it easier to maximize your tax savings. Digitizing your financial documents ensures that all necessary information is ready when tax season arrives, reducing stress and saving you valuable time.

Regular financial reviews are crucial for keeping your plan on track. Scheduling automated reminders for quarterly or annual check-ins helps you consistently evaluate the effectiveness of your strategies. During these reviews, take the time to assess savings and investment performance, making any necessary adjustments to reflect changes in your personal situation. This proactive approach keeps you flexible and ensures your goals remain relevant and attainable.

Incorporating these automated systems into your routine not only saves time but also enhances your ability to make informed decisions. Relying on technology for daily management allows you to concentrate on larger goals and work toward financial independence. Knowing your finances are under control gives you the freedom to explore other interests and opportunities, leading to a more balanced and fulfilling life.

Automating Saving and Investing for Minimal Effort

Financial independence starts with a solid grasp of your financial goals and **risk tolerance**. Begin by outlining both your short-term and long-term objectives. Short-term goals could include:

- Saving $3,000 for a vacation
- Establishing an emergency fund to cover three to six months of living expenses
- Buying a new gadget for under $500

For long-term aspirations, you might aim to:

- Save for a home with a 20% down payment
- Accumulate $1 million for retirement by age 65
- Set aside $100,000 for a child's four-year college education

Clearly defining these targets creates a structured framework for your planning and helps you prioritize how to allocate your resources.

Understanding your **risk tolerance** is just as crucial. This involves figuring out how much risk you're comfortable taking in your investment portfolio. Think about your age, income stability, and how you feel about market fluctuations. For example, a 30-year-old with a steady job might be more inclined to invest in higher-risk assets like stocks for the potential of greater returns. On the other hand, someone who is 60 and approaching retirement may prefer safer investments like bonds to protect their savings. To assess your risk tolerance, consider how you would react if your investments dropped by 10% in a month. Your response will guide you in shaping an investment strategy that fits your comfort level.

Once you've established your goals and grasped your risk tolerance, it's time to select the right financial tools. The digital landscape offers a variety of apps and platforms to help with saving and investing. Look for tools that feature:

- Automated transfers
- Detailed investment tracking
- Customizable alerts to keep an eye on your finances

Compare costs, user reviews, and platform features to find options that meet your needs. Some platforms may have lower fees but fewer features, while others offer a comprehensive range of services at a higher price.

The next step is to open the necessary accounts, such as savings, investment, and retirement accounts, with your chosen institutions or platforms. Link these accounts to your main checking account for easy and efficient fund transfers. This setup simplifies financial management and minimizes the risk of missing savings opportunities due to manual errors or forgetfulness.

Establish automated transfers and contributions to set your savings and investment plans on autopilot. Decide on a fixed amount or percentage of your income to allocate toward savings and investments each month. For instance, saving 20% of a $5,000 monthly income means transferring $1,000. Schedule these transfers from your checking account to your savings and investment accounts regularly, such as monthly or bi-weekly. This routine ensures consistent saving and investing, allowing you to build wealth over time without constant oversight.

To enhance your investment potential, take advantage of advanced features available on many platforms. Activate options like:

- Portfolio rebalancing
- Dividend reinvestment
- Tax-loss harvesting

These tools can help optimize your returns and maintain your asset allocation. If you prefer a more hands-off approach, consider using *robo-advisors* or managed accounts that handle your portfolio with algorithms tailored to your risk tolerance and financial goals, providing professional management without the high fees associated with traditional advisors.

Regular monitoring and adjustments are key to keeping your financial strategies effective. Set up notifications for account balances, investment performance, and significant market changes to stay informed. Plan to review your savings and investment strategies every few months. During these reviews, make any necessary adjustments to contributions or investment allocations to ensure alignment with your goals. Staying proactive helps your financial plan adapt to changes in your life or the market.

Protecting your financial assets is vital. Enable **two-factor authentication** and other security features for your accounts to prevent unauthorized access. Change your passwords regularly and keep an eye out for any unusual activity. These steps help safeguard your financial information and provide peace of mind.

Utilize educational resources to boost your understanding of personal finance and investing. Many financial platforms offer materials designed to help you make informed decisions and enhance your automation strategies. Staying updated on market trends and financial news ensures your financial plan remains effective and aligned with your goals.

Chapter 13: Balancing Multiple Jobs and Avoiding Burnout

Tip

Maximize your productivity by identifying your peak energy hours and scheduling your most demanding tasks during these times. Use digital tools like Google Calendar and Trello to organize your day, and don't forget to set boundaries—communicate your work hours to others to protect your personal time.

J uggling multiple jobs and side hustles while maintaining a personal life can be quite a challenge, especially in today's rapidly evolving digital economy. With careful planning and effective time management, you can navigate these responsibilities without falling into burnout. Start by establishing clear priorities and managing your time wisely. Develop a detailed daily and weekly schedule that allocates specific time slots for your main job, side hustles, and personal commitments. Allow for some flexibility to handle unexpected changes, but keep the structure solid enough to guide your daily activities.

Digital tools like calendar apps and task management software are invaluable for staying organized. Tools such as **Google Calendar** and **Trello** help you track deadlines, appointments, and tasks, ensuring you remain accountable. Setting reminders and notifications keeps you ahead of your responsibilities and alleviates the stress of last-minute deadlines. Recognizing the times of day when you're most alert and focused can significantly enhance your productivity. Schedule your most important tasks during these peak periods to achieve more in less time.

Implement **time-blocking** to give your full attention to each job or project without overlap. Assign specific blocks of time to different activities and stick to these timeframes as closely as possible. For example, reserve mornings for your primary job, afternoons for a side hustle, and evenings for personal activities. This division of your day helps keep roles and responsibilities distinct, which is key to preventing burnout.

Establishing clear boundaries is crucial for maintaining a healthy work-life balance. Set specific work hours for each position and communicate these limits to employers, clients, and family members. This approach helps manage expectations and ensures you have dedicated time for personal activities and relaxation. Creating a dedicated workspace that minimizes distractions can further enhance your focus and productivity. Whether you choose a home office or a quiet corner in a coffee shop, having a designated area for work helps you mentally separate professional tasks from your personal life.

Learning to say no to additional commitments that could overwhelm your schedule is an essential skill. While it may be tempting to accept every opportunity, taking on too much can lead to increased stress and a higher risk of burnout. Carefully assess each new opportunity, considering its impact on your current workload and personal life. If it doesn't align with your priorities or financial goals, it's perfectly acceptable to decline.

Look for ways to simplify and delegate tasks to conserve time and energy. Identify what can be automated or outsourced, such as using apps for social media scheduling or hiring freelancers for specific projects. This allows you to concentrate on high-priority tasks that require your direct attention. Regularly evaluate how each side hustle contributes to your financial goals. If a particular venture isn't yielding enough profit or satisfaction, consider scaling back or letting it go to make space for more rewarding activities.

To effectively prevent burnout and maintain motivation, weave self-care and wellness practices into your daily routine. Schedule short, regular breaks throughout your workday—these can be as brief as five minutes. Step away from your desk, take a brisk walk, or engage in mindfulness exercises like focused breathing or body scans. These activities help clear your mind and restore energy, allowing you to return to tasks feeling refreshed and more productive.

Getting enough sleep, eating well, and staying active are essential for both physical and mental health. Aim for **7-9 hours** of uninterrupted sleep each night to support cognitive function and physical recovery. A balanced diet rich in **fruits**, **vegetables**, **lean proteins**, and **whole grains** provides the vitamins and minerals needed for energy and overall well-being. Regular physical activity—such as:

- a 30-minute jog
- a yoga class
- strength training at the gym

can lower stress and elevate your mood by releasing endorphins.

Relaxation techniques like *meditation, yoga,* or *deep-breathing exercises* help reduce stress and foster a sense of calm, making it easier to manage multiple responsibilities. Set aside a specific time each day for these practices, and gradually increase the duration as you become more comfortable with them.

Set realistic goals and acknowledge your achievements to keep motivation high. Break larger objectives into smaller, actionable tasks and assign achievable deadlines to each one. This approach transforms overwhelming projects into manageable steps and provides a clear plan. Regularly check your progress and celebrate both major milestones and small wins. Recognizing these successes reinforces your sense of accomplishment and motivates you to keep moving forward.

A strong support network is invaluable when juggling multiple jobs and side hustles. Connect with peers or mentors who understand your unique challenges and can offer guidance or encouragement. Joining communities or groups that share your interests creates opportunities to exchange experiences and insights. These relationships provide motivation and support, helping you stay focused and resilient.

Take time to reflect on your workload and mental well-being to catch early signs of burnout. Evaluate your commitments and consider whether they align with your long-term goals and personal health. If something no longer serves you, adjust your routine or commitments as needed. Staying flexible helps you remain on a path that supports overall health and happiness.

Passion projects can reignite motivation and creativity. Set aside time for activities or projects that bring you joy and fulfillment, such as *painting, writing,* or *volunteering.* These pursuits offer a refreshing break from work-related tasks and can inspire fresh ideas and perspectives in other areas of your life.

Chapter 14: Overcoming Financial Setbacks and Building Resilience

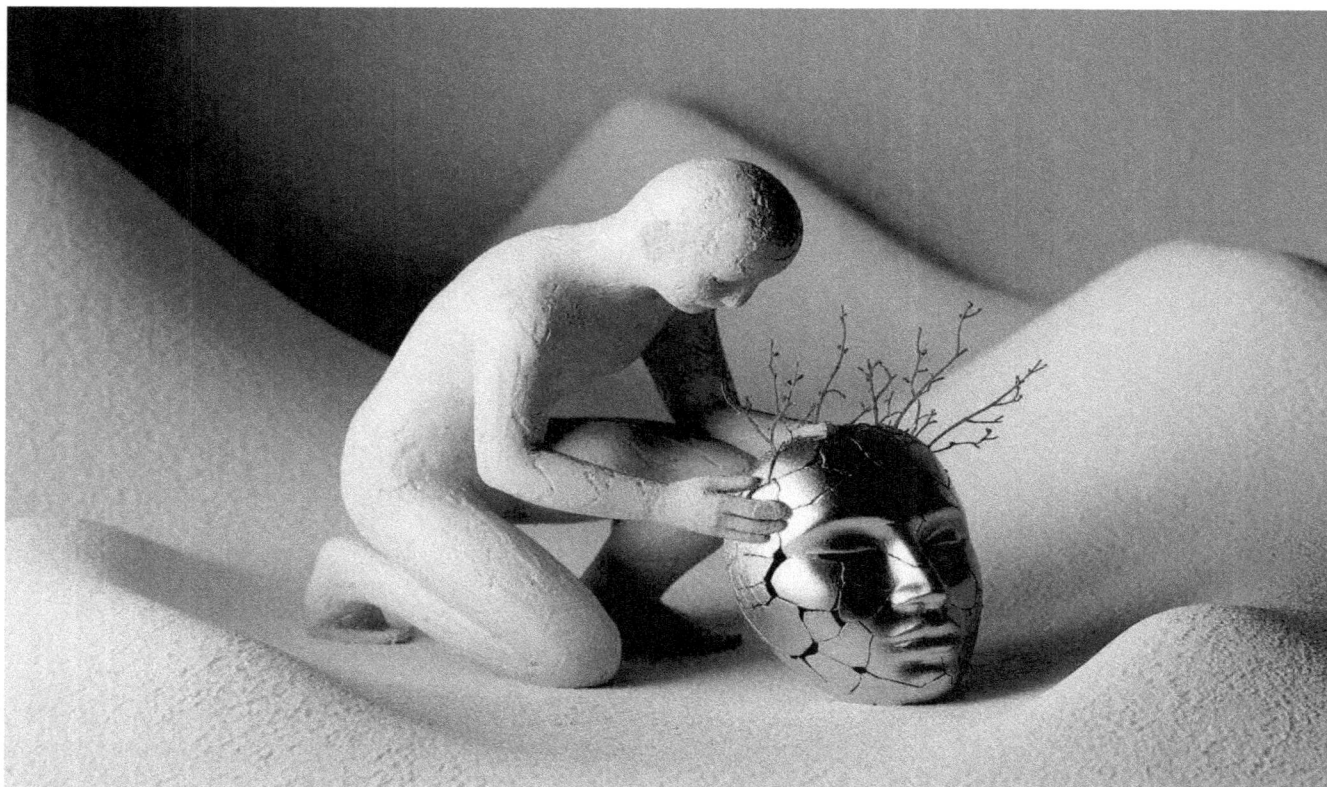

Tip

When facing a financial setback, don't go it alone—reach out to mentors or online communities for advice and support. Many Millennials and Gen Z have navigated similar challenges and can offer practical tips or emotional encouragement. Sharing your experience not only helps you find solutions faster but also builds a network that can open doors to new opportunities and resources as you recover and grow.

F inancial setbacks can be tough, but they also present a valuable chance to reassess your strategies, gain new insights, and boost your financial knowledge. Begin by thoroughly analyzing the situation. Pinpoint the root causes, which may include external factors like a recession causing job loss or unexpected medical bills that deplete your savings, as well as internal missteps such as overspending on non-essentials or making unwise investment choices. Collect quantitative data from your financial statements and seek feedback from trusted advisors or mentors who can provide objective perspectives. This analysis will clarify the specific issues behind the setback and give you a clearer view of your financial status.

Once you have a solid understanding of the situation, develop a detailed, step-by-step action plan to address immediate challenges. Prioritize repaying **high-interest debts** first, as these can accumulate quickly and worsen your situation. Take a critical look at your monthly expenses to identify areas for cutbacks, such as:

- Canceling unused subscriptions
- Reducing dining out
- Limiting entertainment costs

Explore ways to boost your income through part-time work or freelance opportunities. Online platforms like *Upwork* or *Fiverr* can help you leverage your skills and create a viable source of supplemental income.

Establishing clear, measurable goals is crucial during this recovery phase. Define both short-term and long-term objectives that focus on rebuilding savings and enhancing stability. Short-term goals might include:

- Saving a specific amount each month
- Paying off a particular debt within a set timeframe

Long-term goals could involve:

- Building an emergency fund that covers three to six months of living expenses
- Creating a diversified investment portfolio to mitigate risk

Building resilience is key to overcoming setbacks. Start by establishing an emergency fund to cover unexpected expenses. Aim to save enough to cover three to six months of living costs, which will act as a financial cushion and provide peace of mind. Diversifying your income streams also enhances stability. Consider exploring various income-generating activities, such as freelance work, real estate investments, or creating passive income through digital products.

Regularly review and adjust your plans to stay responsive to changing circumstances. This proactive approach will help you navigate potential challenges and make informed decisions about your future. Treat setbacks as valuable learning experiences. Reflect on the lessons learned and think about how these insights can inform your financial decisions. Maintain a positive attitude toward calculated risk-taking and innovation, recognizing that well-considered risks can lead to significant rewards.

Seeking support and resources is a vital step in the recovery process. Collaborate with advisors, mentors, or support groups to gain insights and strategies for overcoming obstacles. Utilize educational resources like financial literacy books, online courses, or workshops to deepen your understanding of management and enhance your decision-making skills. Connecting with a community of peers who have faced similar challenges can also provide valuable support and practical recovery strategies.

Chapter 15: Retirement Planning for Millennials and Gen Z

Tip

Start your retirement savings as early as possible—even small, consistent contributions can grow into a substantial nest egg thanks to compound interest. Prioritize capturing your employer's 401(k) match and diversify your investments to balance risk and reward as your goals evolve.

Retirement planning is essential for Millennials and Gen Z, especially in a world where traditional job security is becoming less dependable. Begin by looking into the various retirement accounts available to you. Individual Retirement Accounts (IRAs) come in two primary types: Traditional and Roth, each with unique features, tax implications, and benefits designed to fit different financial situations and aspirations.

Traditional IRAs allow you to contribute pre-tax dollars, which can lower your taxable income for the year. For instance, if you contribute $6,000, your taxable income decreases by that amount, potentially reducing your tax bill. Keep in mind, though, that this tax advantage is deferred—you'll pay taxes on withdrawals during retirement. In 2023, the contribution limit is $6,500, or $7,500 if you're 50 or older, and these limits may increase annually to keep pace with inflation.

Roth IRAs, in contrast, are funded with after-tax dollars. You pay taxes on your contributions now, but if you meet certain criteria, your withdrawals in retirement are tax-free. This can be particularly beneficial if you anticipate being in a higher tax bracket when you retire. The contribution limits align with those of Traditional IRAs, but higher earners may face restrictions. In 2023, eligibility begins to phase out at $138,000 for single filers and $218,000 for married couples filing jointly.

Starting an IRA early can be a game-changer due to the power of compound interest. Your investment grows over time as you earn returns on both your initial contributions and the interest they generate. For example, if you contribute $500 a month to an IRA starting at age 25, with an average annual return of 7%, you could see a balance exceeding $1 million by age 65. This illustrates how early and consistent contributions can lead to substantial long-term growth.

401(k) plans, which are employer-sponsored retirement accounts, come with several advantages, including the opportunity to receive matching contributions from your employer. Many companies match a portion of your contributions, adding extra funds to your savings. For instance, if your employer matches 50% of your contributions up to 6% of your salary, contributing at least 6% ensures you capture the full match, which can significantly boost your savings.

Understanding how **vesting** works is crucial. This process determines how long you need to remain with your employer before fully owning the company's contributions to your 401(k). Your own contributions are always yours, but employer contributions may become yours gradually, typically over three to five years.

401(k) plans also offer tax benefits. Contributions are made with pre-tax dollars, reducing your taxable income, and investments grow tax-deferred until withdrawal. When you take money out, it's taxed as ordinary income. Withdrawing funds before age 59½ usually incurs a 10% penalty, which can diminish your retirement savings.

To make the most of your 401(k), consider the following:

- Contribute enough to receive the full employer match
- Review the investment options available in your plan

- Diversify your investments across different assets to mitigate risk and enhance growth potential

Assessing your retirement needs is another vital step. Start with a thorough review of your personal finances to clarify your goals. Think about the lifestyle you envision, anticipated healthcare costs, and how inflation might impact your plans. Establishing a specific savings target provides you with a clear objective. Determine how much you need to save each month to reach that target, considering your current savings, expected investment returns, and the time remaining to save.

Diversification is a fundamental strategy for achieving long-term financial security, especially for Millennials and Gen Z who are navigating a complex and ever-evolving economic landscape. By spreading investments across various asset classes—such as **stocks**, **bonds**, **real estate**, and alternatives like *commodities* or *cryptocurrencies*—you can mitigate the impact of downturns in any single market. For example, if stocks decline by 15%, gains from bonds yielding 3% or real estate appreciating by 5% can help cushion losses and safeguard your overall capital.

Asset allocation is about intentionally distributing investments among different classes to find the right balance between **risk** and **reward**, tailored to your unique financial goals and risk tolerance. While many investors adhere to the **60/40 rule**—allocating 60% to equities and 40% to fixed income—this mix can be adjusted based on your personal circumstances, investment timelines, and current market conditions. To keep your portfolio aligned with these goals, regular rebalancing is essential. For instance, if equities rise to 70% of your portfolio due to market gains, selling some stocks and reallocating those funds into bonds can help restore the desired 60/40 split.

Risk management is crucial in retirement planning. Financial products like **life** and **disability insurance** provide a safety net against unexpected events that could jeopardize your stability. **Annuities** can also offer a reliable income stream during retirement, which is particularly valuable in an unpredictable job market, alleviating concerns about job loss or fluctuating income.

To adapt financial plans for the future, it's important to stay attuned to new trends and investment opportunities. Continuous education about financial developments—such as **sustainable investing** and **digital currencies**—is vital. Sustainable investing emphasizes supporting companies with strong environmental, social, and governance (ESG) practices, catering to the growing desire among investors to align their portfolios with ethical values. Digital currencies like *Bitcoin* and *Ethereum* present new avenues for diversification, though they come with heightened volatility and risk. Understanding these trends and their implications for investment strategies is essential for keeping pace with a changing economy.

Retirement planning demands flexibility, as personal circumstances, economic shifts, and evolving preferences can all influence financial goals. Regularly reviewing and updating your plans ensures they remain aligned with your long-term objectives. Major life events, such as marriage or the arrival of a child, may require adjustments to your savings strategies. Additionally, changes in the economy, like fluctuations in interest rates or new tax laws, might prompt a reassessment of your investment approach to optimize returns.

Sustainable Wealth Strategies for Every Generation

Millennials and Gen Z encounter distinct challenges and opportunities as they strive for financial independence in today's rapidly evolving economic landscape. To build and maintain wealth sustainably, it's essential to adopt strategies that resonate with the values and realities of these generations. Establishing solid financial habits begins with consistent saving; setting up automatic transfers to savings and investment accounts can seamlessly integrate this practice into your routine. Living below your means not only enhances your ability to save but also creates a financial cushion that fosters security and peace of mind.

Creating an **emergency fund** is a cornerstone of financial stability. Ideally, this fund should cover three to six months of essential living expenses, serving as a safety net against unforeseen events like job loss or unexpected medical bills. By prioritizing this reserve, you shield yourself from financial shocks that could derail your long-term wealth-building efforts.

Personal development and skill enhancement are also crucial for sustainable wealth accumulation. The job market is evolving rapidly due to technological advancements, making ongoing education and skill development vital. Engaging in online courses, attending workshops, and obtaining relevant certifications can boost your employability and adaptability, enhancing your competitiveness across various careers. Soft skills such as effective communication, adaptability, and problem-solving are particularly valuable, as they are applicable across numerous industries and roles.

Opting for **environmentally** and **socially responsible investments** can further bolster sustainable wealth building. Investing in companies and funds that adhere to environmental, social, and governance (ESG) criteria allows you to align your investments with your values while potentially reaping long-term financial rewards. The rising interest in impact investing, which seeks positive social or environmental outcomes alongside financial returns, offers another avenue to harmonize financial goals with ethical principles.

Exploring innovative financial products is vital for diversifying income sources and investment portfolios. Consider the following options:

- Peer-to-peer lending platforms
- Micro-investing apps
- Crowdfunding opportunities

These resonate with generational values and introduce fresh ways to engage in the financial market. Digital assets like cryptocurrencies also present exciting growth opportunities, but it's essential to understand the associated risks and make informed decisions.

Preparing for **intergenerational wealth transfer** is key to long-term preservation. Effective estate planning, which includes establishing wills, trusts, and beneficiary designations, ensures a smooth transfer of assets while minimizing tax burdens. Encouraging open family discussions about financial goals and inheritance plans is crucial for fostering financial literacy and readiness across generations.

Chapter 16: Real Stories of Financial Freedom

In the heart of bustling New York City, we find Sarah, a 28-year-old Millennial who has achieved financial independence through the gig economy. After graduating with a degree in graphic design, she faced a saturated job market that made securing a traditional 9-to-5 position challenging. Instead of succumbing to the pressure, Sarah embraced the flexibility of freelancing. By utilizing platforms like Upwork and Fiverr, she built a diverse client base, offering design services to businesses across various sectors worldwide. To navigate the ups and downs of her income, Sarah created a detailed budget that reflected her fluctuating monthly earnings and prioritized saving during high-income months, consistently setting aside at least 20% during peak periods. Her journey illustrates how adaptability and strategic financial planning are vital for achieving financial freedom.

Across the Atlantic, in the vibrant city of Berlin, we meet Alex, a Gen Z entrepreneur who turned a passion for sustainable fashion into a thriving business. At just 24, he identified a market gap for eco-friendly clothing that also looked great. With a modest savings of €5,000 and a small loan of €10,000 from a local startup incubator, Alex launched an online store. The early days required resilience and a smart approach to networking. He made it a point to attend at least five industry events each year and effectively leveraged social media platforms, building a brand that resonated with environmentally conscious consumers. This experience highlights how innovation and community engagement are essential for entrepreneurial success.

In the digital realm, we encounter Jamie, a 26-year-old from San Francisco, who has skillfully harnessed technology for wealth-building. What started as a casual interest in *cryptocurrencies* blossomed into a significant income stream through diligent research and calculated investments. By using platforms like **Coinbase** and **Binance** to navigate the volatile crypto market, Jamie made informed decisions by consistently evaluating market trends and risk factors. His experience showcases the potential of digital tools in modern wealth-building and emphasizes the importance of ongoing education and risk management strategies.

In the serene landscapes of rural Vermont, we find Emma, a Millennial who achieved financial freedom through meaningful lifestyle changes. After years of urban living, she decided to downsize and relocate to a more affordable area. Embracing minimalist principles reduced her living expenses by about **40%**, allowing her to concentrate on long-term financial goals, such as saving for retirement and investing in a diversified portfolio. Emma underwent a significant mindset shift, prioritizing experiences over material possessions. Her story serves as a powerful example of intentional living and strategic planning on the path to financial independence.

In the tech-savvy city of Austin, Texas, we meet Ryan, a Gen Z individual who has consistently upskilled to stay competitive in the ever-evolving job market. He began his career as a customer service representative and dedicated time to online courses and certifications, ultimately transitioning into a lucrative role in data analysis with a salary increase of over **50%**. His commitment to personal development and adaptability illustrates the profound impact of continuous learning on financial success.

The story of the Martinez family from Miami highlights how effective planning can secure intergenerational wealth transfer. By engaging in comprehensive financial planning, they educated younger generations about financial literacy, ensuring a smooth transition of assets. Their approach included:

- Establishing trusts and wills
- Minimizing tax liabilities through strategic gifting
- Fostering open discussions about financial goals and responsibilities

This experience underscores the importance of proactive estate planning and financial education for preserving wealth across generations.

Key Takeaway

Financial freedom isn't a one-size-fits-all journey. Whether through freelancing, entrepreneurship, digital investing, lifestyle changes, or upskilling, Millennials and Gen Z can achieve independence by embracing adaptability, continuous learning, and intentional financial planning. The stories in this chapter show that leveraging digital tools, building strong networks, and prioritizing education and strategic saving are essential steps toward lasting wealth in today's evolving economy.

Chapter 17: Roadmap to Financial Independence

Tip

Start your journey to financial independence by automating your savings and investments. Setting up automatic transfers to your savings account or investment platforms ensures you consistently build wealth, even when life gets busy. This simple habit can make a huge difference over time, especially if your income fluctuates. Automation removes the temptation to spend what you intend to save and helps you stay on track with your goals. Remember, consistency is key—let technology work for you!

To achieve financial independence, begin by setting specific, realistic goals that align with your personal values and long-term aspirations. This initial step provides clear direction and motivation, ensuring that every financial decision supports your primary life objectives. Define what financial independence means to you—whether it's traveling frequently, retiring early, or simply establishing a stable foundation. Once you have a clear vision, break it down into concrete, measurable targets. For example, if you aim to save for a house down payment, determine the exact amount needed and establish a timeline for reaching that goal.

Assess your current financial situation to create a detailed profile. Analyze your income, expenses, debts, and assets thoroughly. List all sources of income, including your main job, side gigs, and passive earnings. Track your monthly expenses closely to understand your spending patterns. Separate them into essentials and non-essentials:

- Essentials: rent, groceries
- Non-essentials: dining out, entertainment

This breakdown helps you identify areas where you can cut back and redirect funds toward your goals.

Review your debts and assets by compiling a complete list of outstanding liabilities—credit card balances, student loans, and other obligations—along with their interest rates and minimum payments. Do the same for your assets, including savings accounts, investments, and real estate. This comprehensive overview serves as the foundation for effective planning.

Once you have a clear picture of your finances, create a flexible budget that can accommodate variable income streams common in today's job market. Traditional budgets often rely on a fixed monthly income, but a flexible approach adapts to changes, which is especially useful for freelancers or gig workers. Set a baseline budget to cover essential expenses, then allocate a portion of your income to savings and debt repayment. When your income is higher, increase your savings and make extra debt payments. In months with lower income, focus on covering essentials and meeting your obligations.

Managing debt effectively is crucial for your strategy. Prioritize paying off high-interest debts first, as these can accumulate quickly and hinder your progress toward independence. You might consider the *avalanche method*, which targets the highest-interest debt first, or the *snowball method*, which pays off the smallest debt to build momentum. Explore consolidation options that could simplify payments and lower interest rates.

Establish an emergency fund to safeguard against financial surprises. Aim to save enough to cover at least three to six months of living expenses. This fund acts as a safety net, providing stability and peace of mind in the face of unexpected events like job loss or medical emergencies. Start with a small, manageable monthly contribution and increase it as your finances improve.

Expanding your income sources can significantly enhance your journey to financial independence. The digital economy offers numerous opportunities to earn extra money through freelance work, side gigs, and passive income streams. Leverage your skills and interests to provide services on platforms like Upwork or Fiverr, or consider creating digital products such as e-books or online courses. Investing in stocks, real estate, or peer-to-peer lending can also generate passive income that grows over time.

Ongoing skill development and adaptability are essential for maintaining and growing your income streams. The job market is constantly evolving, so staying competitive requires a commitment to lifelong learning. Take online courses, attend workshops, and earn certifications that enhance your skills and open new opportunities. Staying proactive and flexible will help you navigate the challenges of today's economy and continue building wealth.

Strategic investing is the cornerstone of achieving financial independence, beginning with a solid understanding of traditional investment vehicles. **Stocks**, **bonds**, and **real estate** form the backbone of most portfolios. Stocks represent ownership in a company and can yield significant returns, though they come with higher volatility and risk. Bonds, in contrast, are fixed-income securities that typically offer steadier but lower returns, making them a good fit for those who prefer a more cautious approach. Real estate can generate income through rent and may appreciate in value over time, making it a vital component of a diversified strategy.

In addition to these traditional options, newer avenues like **cryptocurrencies**, **index funds**, and **micro-investing platforms** have gained popularity. Cryptocurrencies such as *Bitcoin* and *Ethereum* carry high risk but also the potential for substantial rewards, necessitating careful research and a solid grasp of market fluctuations. Index funds track the performance of a specific market index, providing a more stable and diversified investment approach, often with lower fees than actively managed funds. Micro-investing platforms enable individuals to start investing with small amounts of money, creating opportunities for those with limited resources.

Thorough research and risk assessment are crucial when exploring these options. Understanding market dynamics, reviewing historical performance, and staying informed about potential future trends for each investment type are all essential steps. **Diversifying** investments across various asset classes and sectors helps manage risk and mitigates the impact of any single investment's poor performance.

Establishing and managing retirement accounts is a key aspect of financial planning. Individual Retirement Accounts (IRAs) and 401(k)s provide tax advantages that can help your savings grow over time.

- Traditional IRAs allow you to contribute pre-tax income, reducing your taxable income for the year.

- Roth IRAs use after-tax contributions and permit tax-free withdrawals in retirement.
- Many employers offer 401(k) plans, often with matching contributions that can significantly enhance retirement savings.

The power of **compound interest** can greatly accelerate growth. Reinvesting earnings allows your money to grow at an increasing rate. For instance, investing $10,000 at a 7% annual return will grow to approximately $19,672 in 10 years, $38,697 in 20 years, and $76,123 in 30 years, all thanks to the magic of compounding.

Financial literacy is vital for making informed decisions. Stay current on market trends, regulatory changes, and economic shifts that could influence your strategy. Utilize financial news sites, podcasts, and books to enhance your knowledge. Joining investment clubs or online forums can also provide valuable insights and help you expand your network.

A personalized wealth-building plan aligns your saving, investing, and spending habits with your financial goals. Set clear, measurable objectives and develop a structured plan to achieve them. Regularly review and adjust the plan to reflect changes in your finances or the market.

www.ingramcontent.com/pod-product-compliance
Lightning Source LLC
Chambersburg PA
CBHW081746200326
41597CB00024B/4403